FLOWERING UNDER STRESS

It's strange to remember the moment you first heard the word "pandemic." I mean, now that the word is as familiar to us as our own names. I remember it as a falling feeling, one of profound unreality, like the tumble Alice takes down that rabbit hole. Just when you thought you couldn't fall any further, you kept going. Most of us just fell. But if you were like Alice—or like Ana Prvački—after a while, you were able not only to fall but to notice things as you fell. Your own body. The things around you. Words and their meanings. The long, bewitching ears of the white rabbit himself!

This book is a product of that surreal time in all our lives. Within it, you will find:

1. Things
2. Bodies
3. Words (but not "pandemic")
4. States
5. Ideas

Of course, you will find such things in your own life everywhere you look and all the time, but in this book—as it was in the pandemic—they all seem to be suddenly isolated, the one from the next, starkly surrounded by white space, without history, without memory, as if newly born into our consciousness. Frozen in an eternal, traumatic present.

During the pandemic, objects shimmered and vibrated, mostly because in your fugue state, you were often to be found sitting around just staring at them, paying them more attention than you ever had in your life. You'd never known your home so intimately, nor been so familiar with the various items inside it. Frying pan. Slippers. Pillow. Bath. In the absence of people and landscapes, objects became people and landscapes. The borderline between the animate and inanimate became indistinct, like Albrecht Dürer's famous squirming pillows. Things spoke to you. And if you happened to be living alone, well, more often than not, you spoke back.

Sometimes it felt like there was more life in household objects than on Zoom itself. In fact, on that platform, the opposite effect took hold, turning embodied humans into two-dimensional talking heads. With less to look at, we looked intently. And when you went outside on your regulation walk, if there was sun, then it was the sunniest sun ever seen, and if there was rain, every drop was outlined and specific. It was possible to get to the point where you could identify different types of dew. The particular became the universal. A squirrel became "wildlife." A pine tree became "nature." The horizon became very good for your nervous system. Also: the sky. Also: any view of mountains or hills. Of course, you were terribly nervous and all the time. And when you weren't nervous, you were: nauseous, anxious, angry, fearful, sad, and desperate. You languished! Certain words and phrases changed their nature. VANILLA HOMINID. That was one of them. (Although we had a different way of saying it.) Even if you had a Vanilla Hominid living in your house, who had been living there with you for years, you still found yourself beginning to look at him differently, with new eyes. Perhaps this was one of the many perverse side effects of the stupid-haired Vanilla Hominid who ran the American government at the time. The one who went on TV and recommended we all take a dose of bleach for what ailed us. And even from over here, far away, in Europe, we thought: *That Vanilla Hominid is very bad for my nervous system.*

Meanwhile, at the kitchen table, “Hybrid learning” led to *hybridchildren* who could pretend to be attending their Zoom lessons while simultaneously texting, TikToking, or making a study of the acrobatic squirrel walking the tightrope of the laundry line. The hybrid-children’s parents swore to Jeff Bezos and upon all things unholy that they were never, ever going to use Amazon again—but then you went and used Amazon again, didn’t you? Yes, you did. Me too. If only because the arrival of a box could break up a day:

Before box
After box

You opened the door in dressing gown and slippers and realized that you had just ordered a real living hominid to come to your door in the middle of a pandemic to bring you something you really didn’t need, wrapped up in packaging that will last forever. Then you swore never to do it again. The earth is top-heavy because of people like us.

Nature was good for our nervous systems, but even in nature, there were few places for the mind to rest.

We were having hell for breakfast, every day, and then more hell for lunch and dinner, too, and if you stepped outside to take some pleasure in nature—in a horizon or a hill or the shoreline or the sky itself—a moment later you remembered that nature, too, had a virus, a virus called hominids, and it was because of all us hominids (and not just the vanilla ones) that the bees were dying and the earth was top-heavy, for far too many of us at the top were hoarding resources while the bottom half suffered. We tried to burn the shame and sadness of all this like calories, undertaking many new hobbies and fitness goals and community projects, although more often, we languished and we marinated. Imaginary scenarios were constantly on our minds, and the only thing we could imagine was apocalypse. But! The mind is dextrous and can make of anything a metaphor, make of anything a simile. A woman can see herself in the curves of a pepper grinder or the angular gestures of a coffee pot. A woman might lose all sense of her own citified modern reality, seeing herself in a bowl of primal ooze or in the ancient nobbled fertility statues archaeologists sometimes dig out of the earth. Some days were for making art. Others for hiding under a duvet and despairing. But whatever we did, we knew we were like juvenile swans, that is, in a period of radical becoming. Nobody knew what they would be like at the end of it all. (If it ever ended. If it *has* ended.) But everybody knew they would never be the same again. I wish I'd had this book with me during it all, when my nervous system was utterly broken and I didn't know which way was up ...

Yes, I wish I'd had Ana Prvački's exquisite series of existential watercolors with me in that long, dark, seemingly bottomless hole. Whispering in my ear like a homeopathic sea shell:

You are going to be ok
This too shall pass
I am here for you
We are all in this together

Zadie Smith
January 2023, London

WATERCOLORS

Support Shell

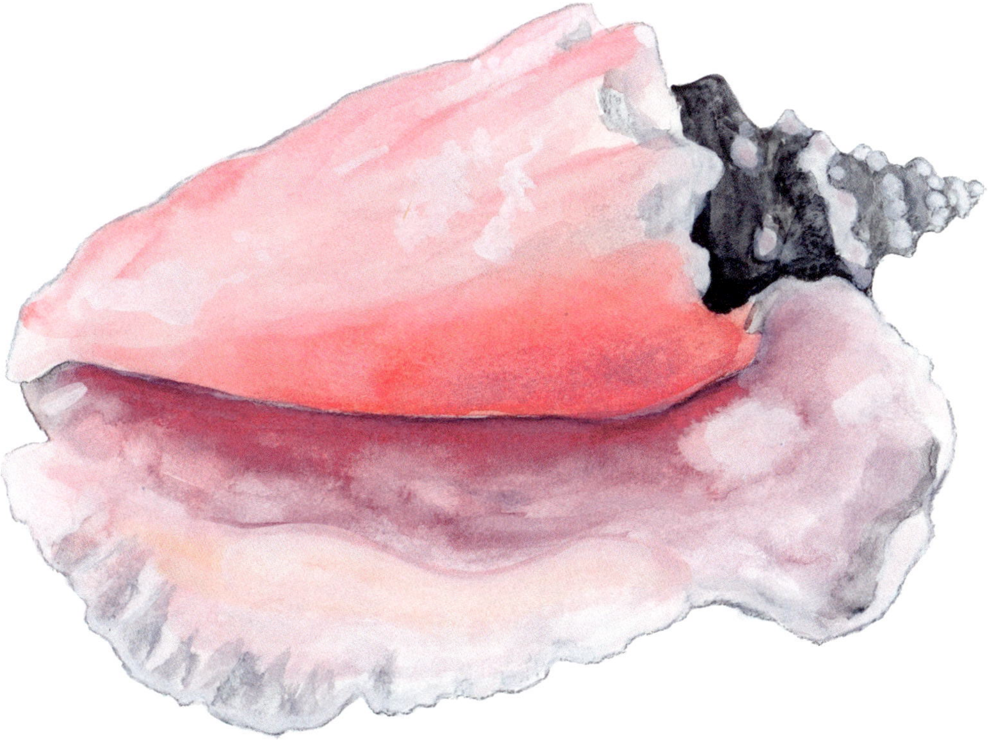

FIND A SEA SHELL AND TRAIN IT TO REASSURE YOU

SUGGESTED LINES:

YOU ARE GOING TO BE OK
THIS TOO SHALL PASS
I AM HERE FOR YOU
WE ARE ALL IN THIS TOGETHER

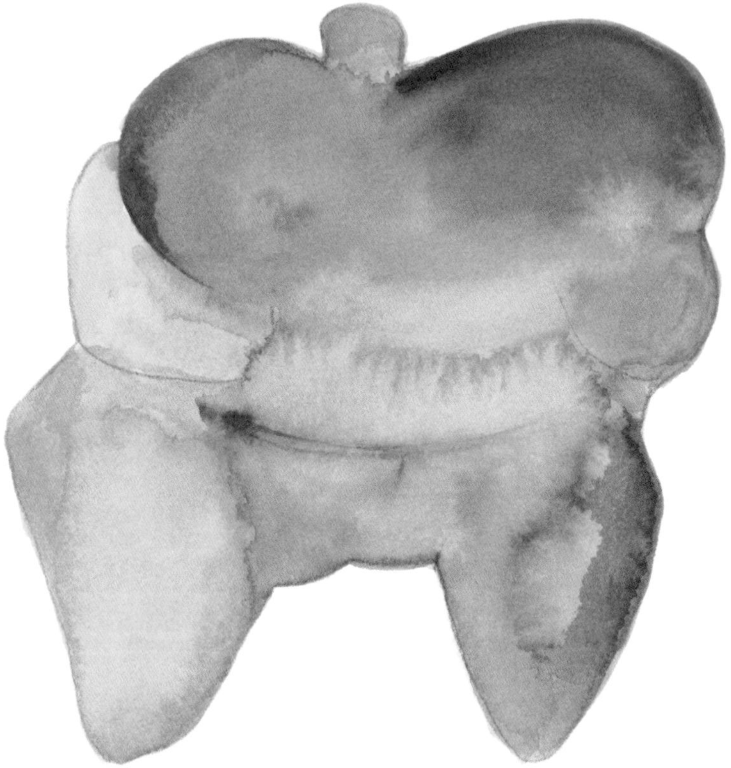

Prehistoric

Sexually Mature Queen

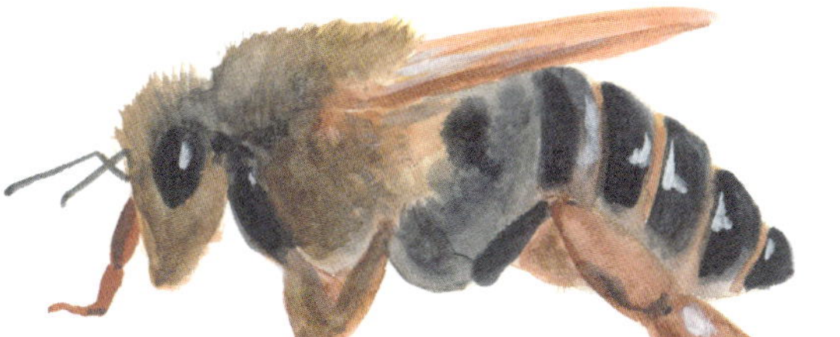

Moss

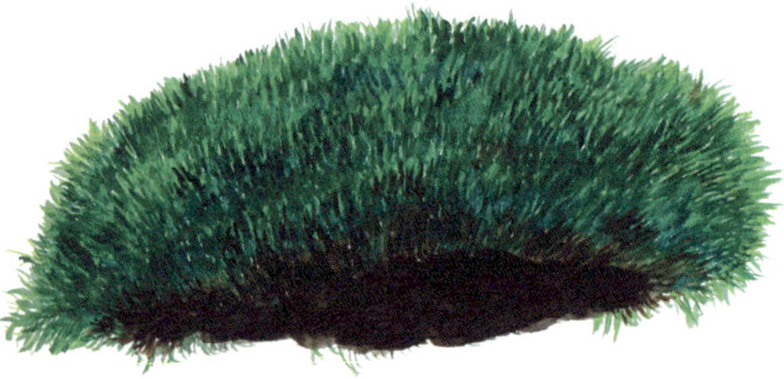

Playmate

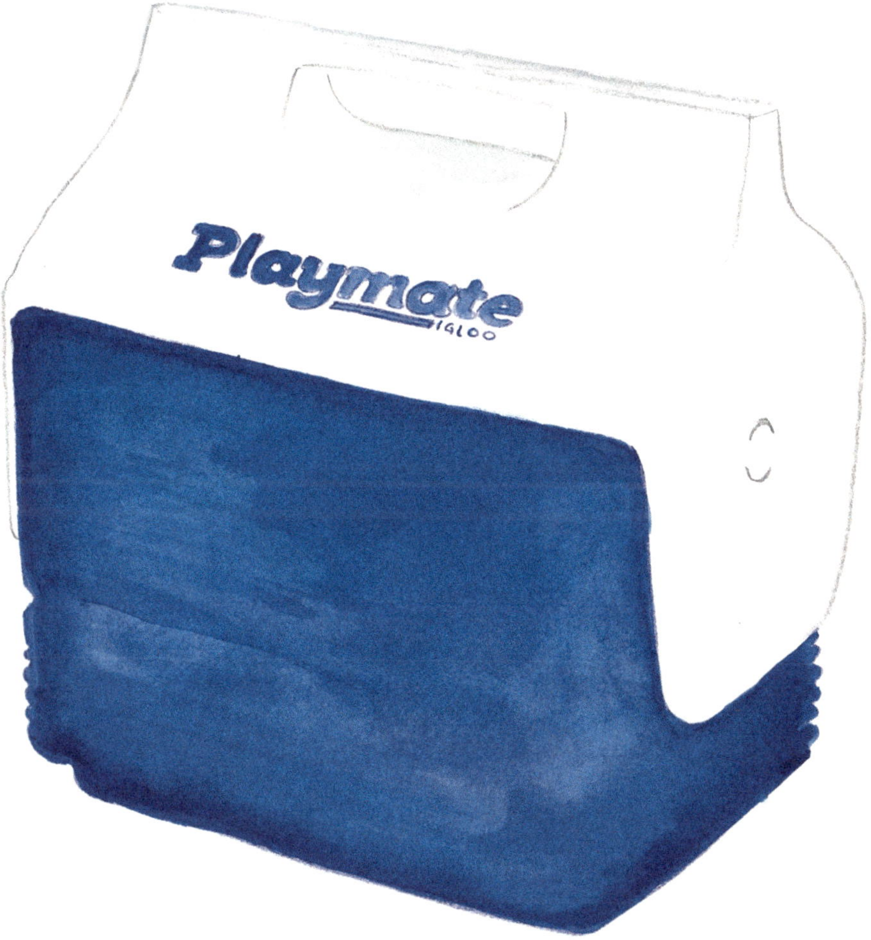

Zebra

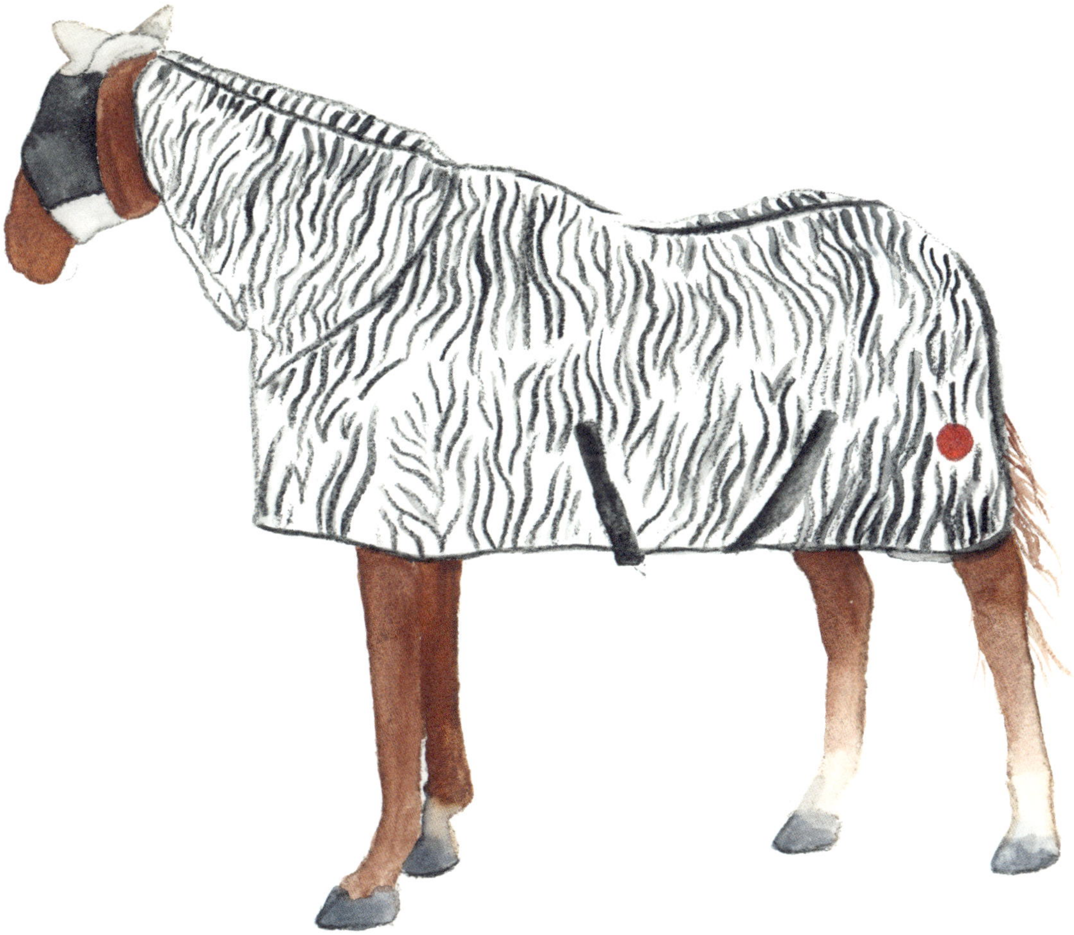

Wild Watercolor Fire

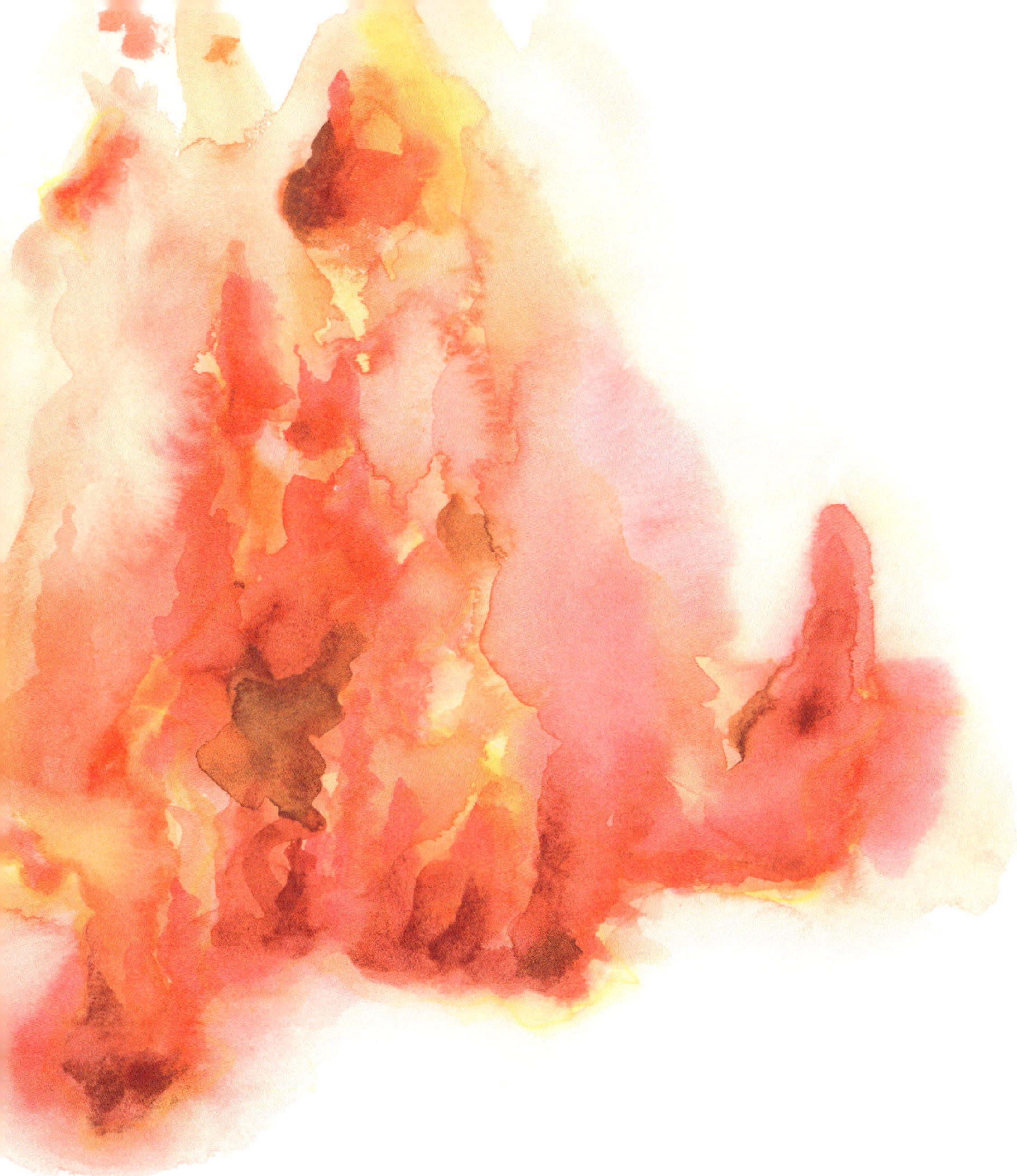

ATERCOLOUR FIRE

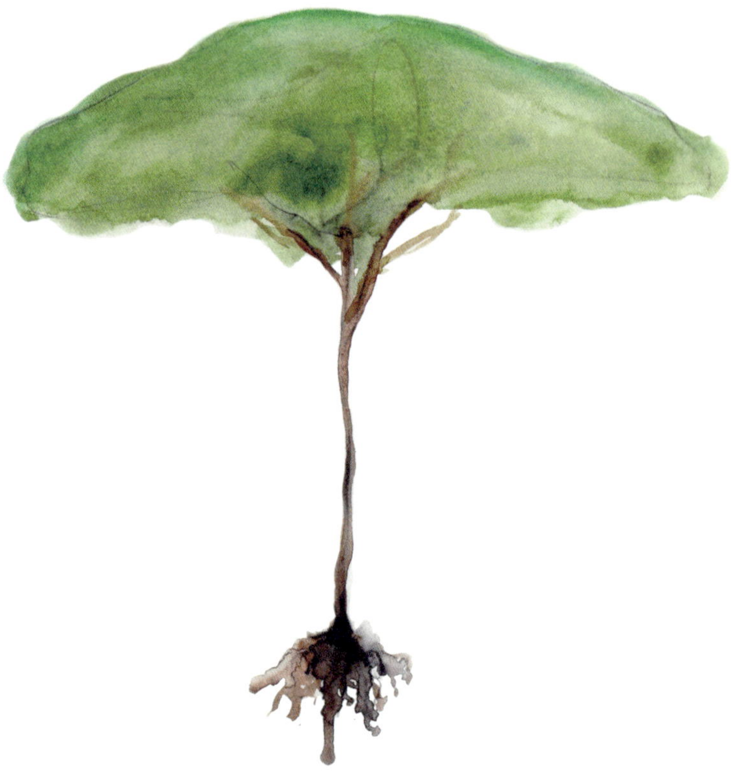

Pinus Piñata

Juvenile Swan

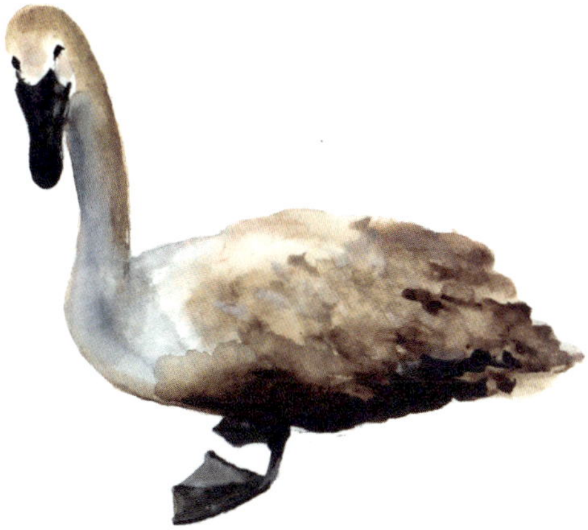

Wallpaper with Mosquito Blood Pattern

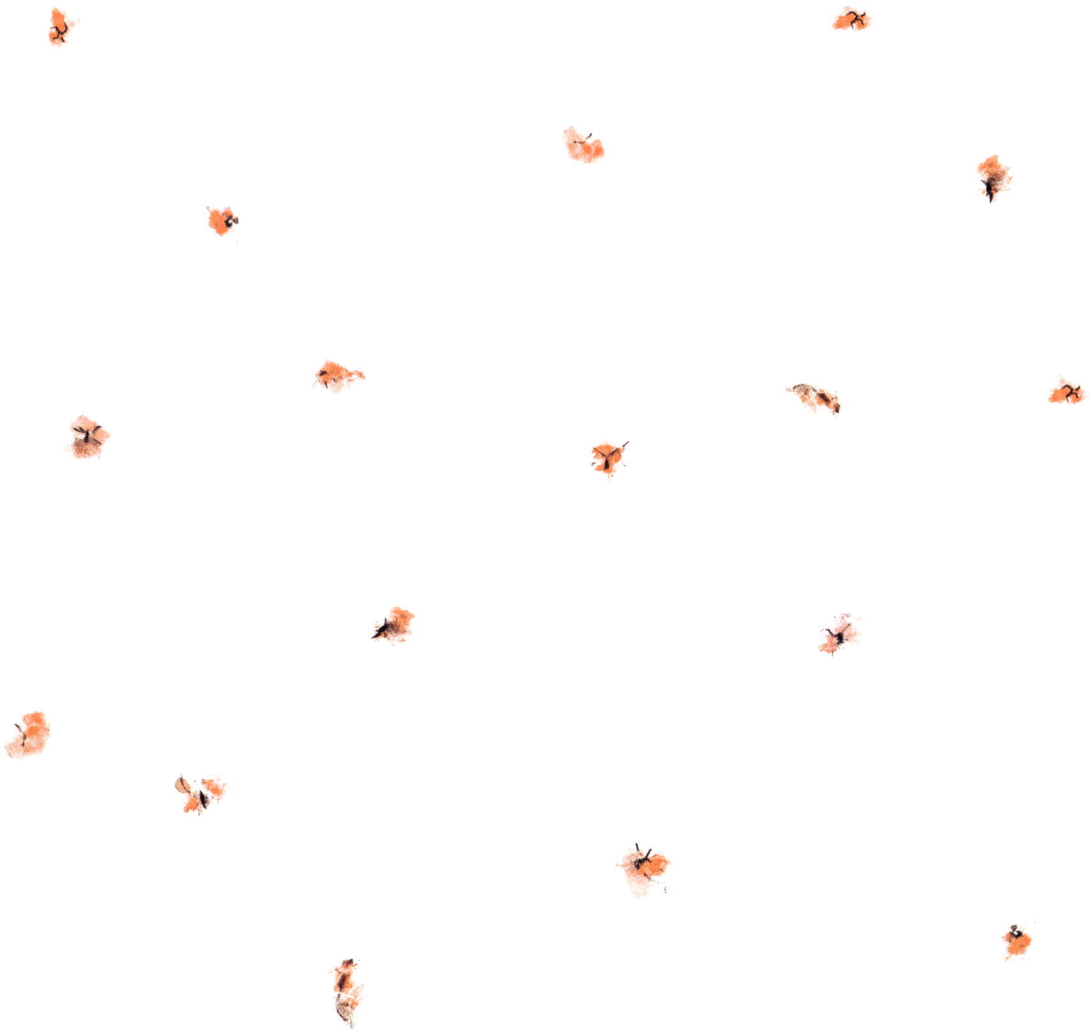

WALLPAPER WITH MOSQUITO BLOOD PATTERN

Virtual hives are the new crypto currency!

What exactly is nature sovereignty and how to invest in it?

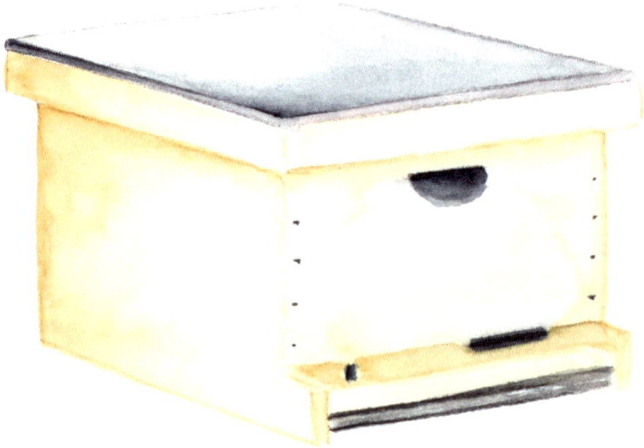

Virtual Hives are the New Cryptocurrency

So Important for Your Nervous System

Dexterity

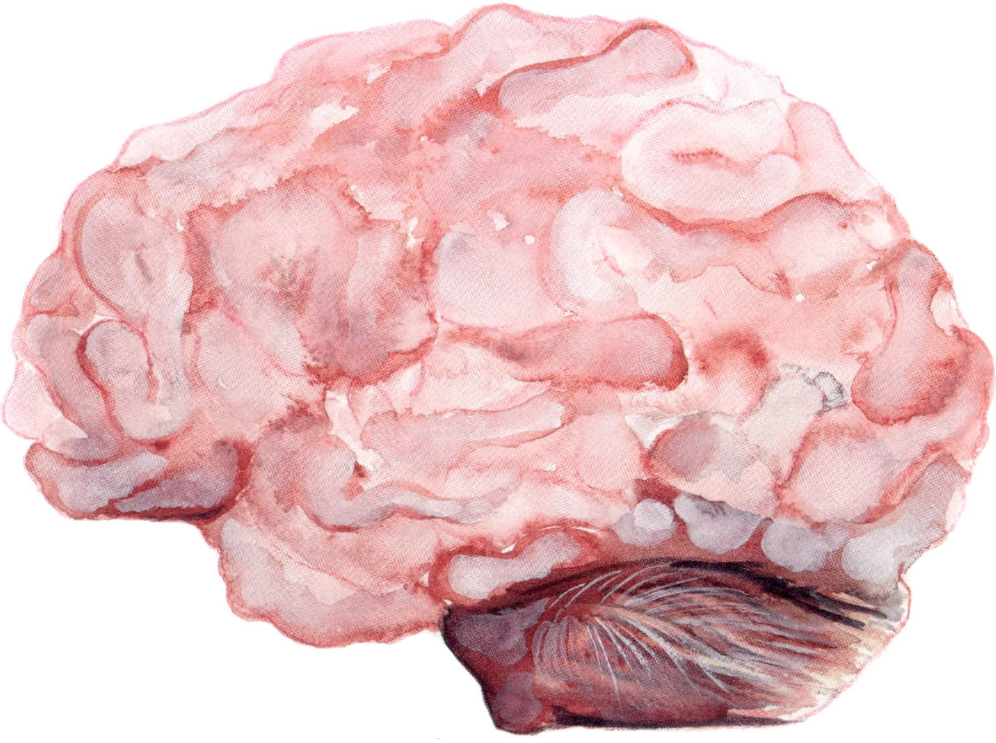

D E X T E R I T Y

Bunny Ears

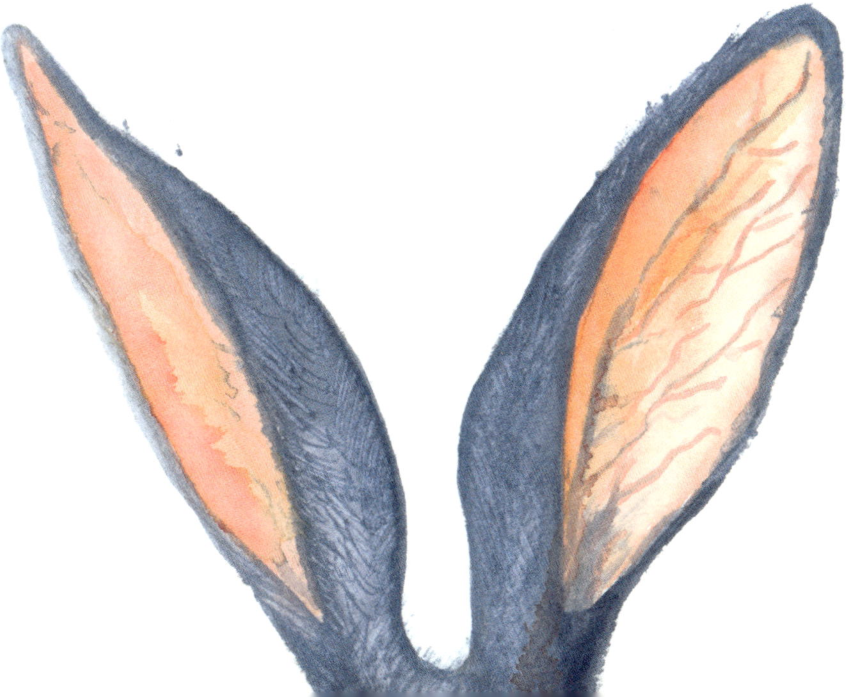

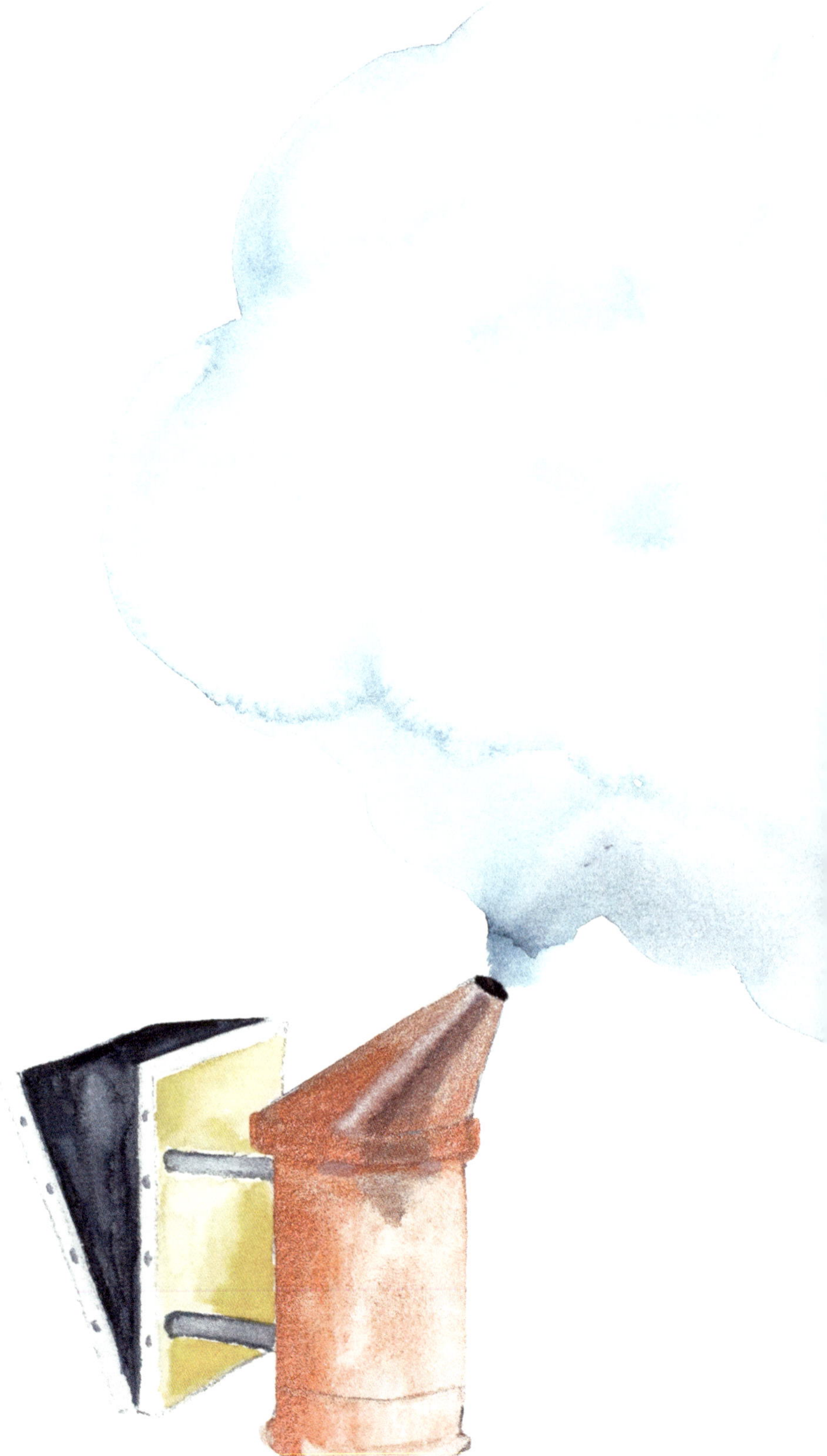

Smoke

Noah’s Fridge, 2021

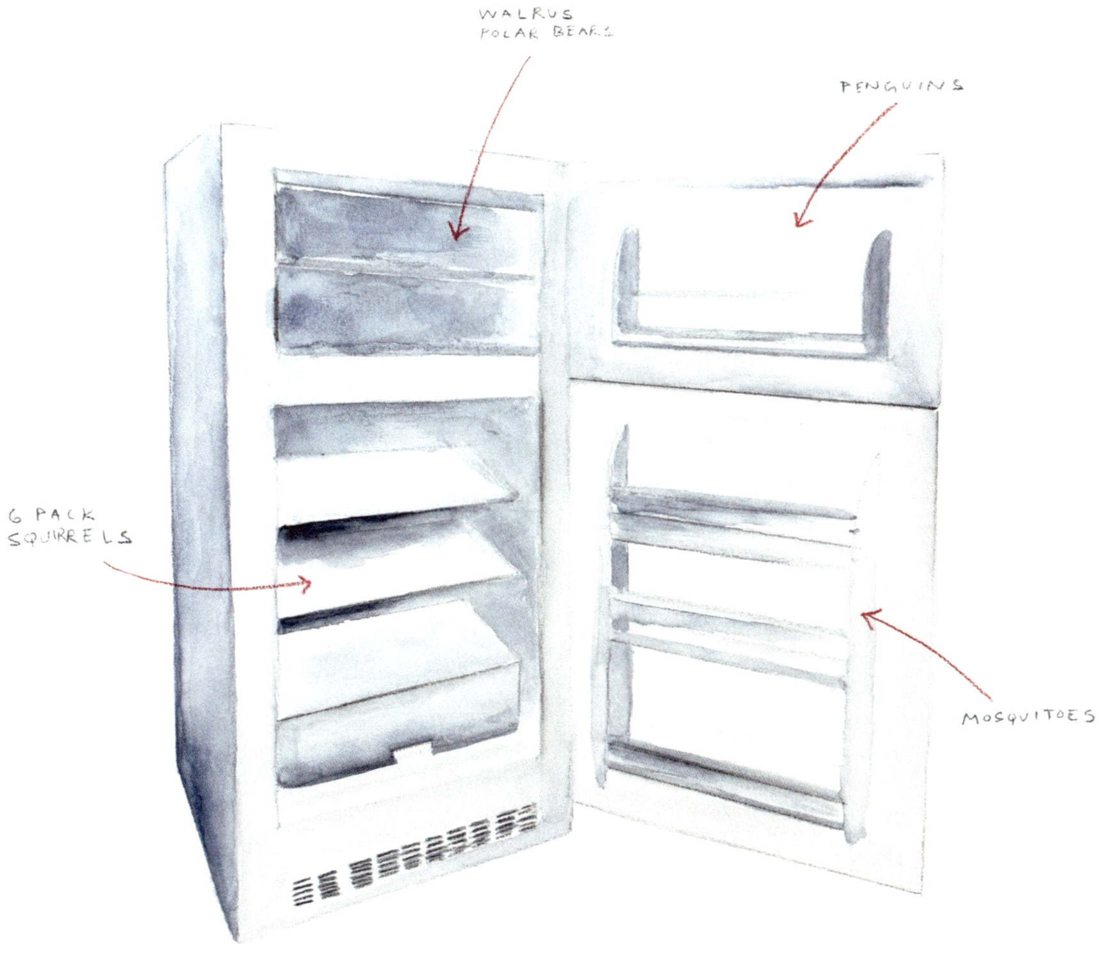

NOAH'S FRIDGE 2021

The Airborne Future Requires Moisture to Live

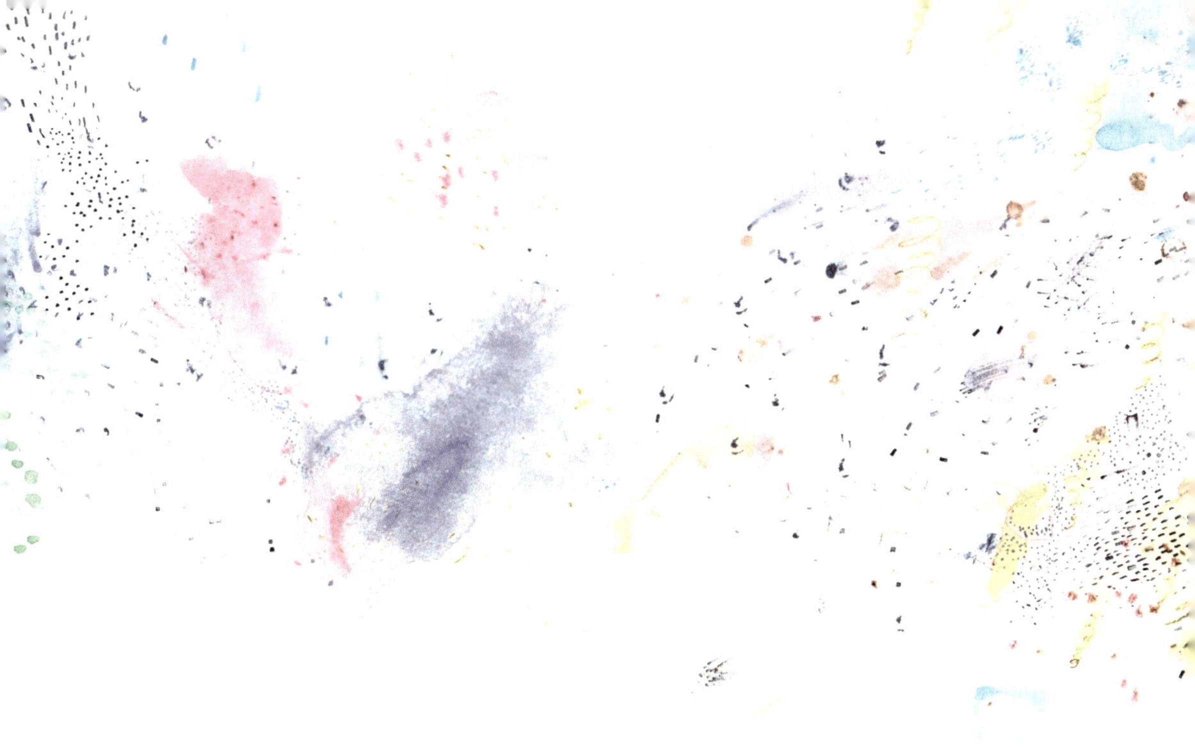

THE AIRBORNE FUTURE REQUIRES MOISTURE TO LIVE

Sacrum and Coccyx with Neolithic Arrow

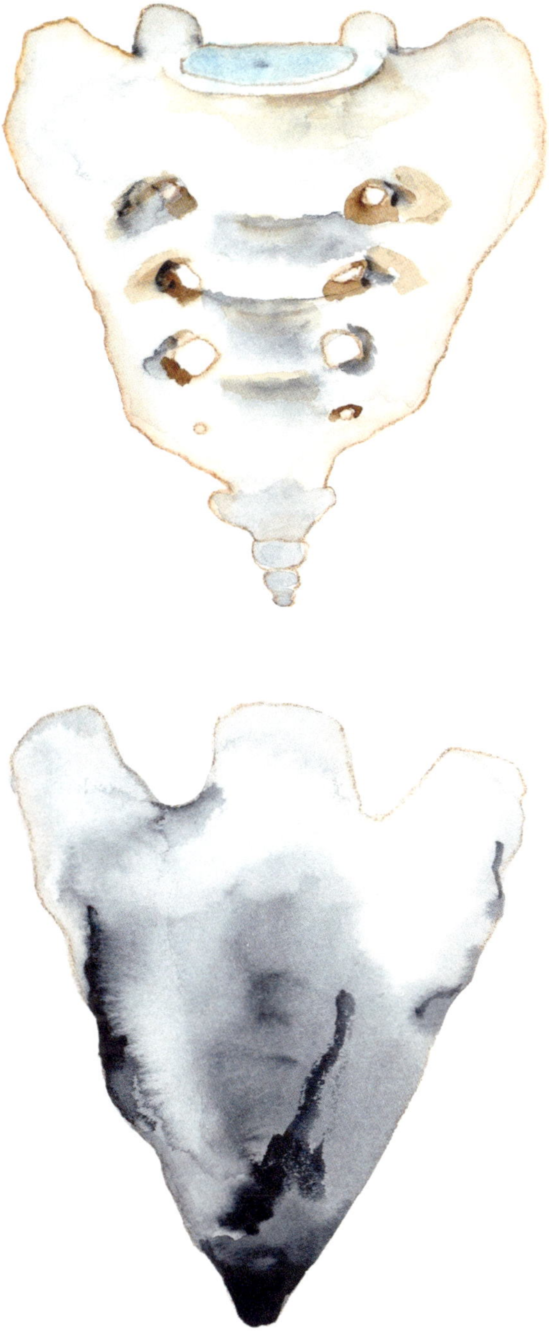

SACRUM AND COCCYX WITH NEOLITHIC ARROW

Hell for Breakfast

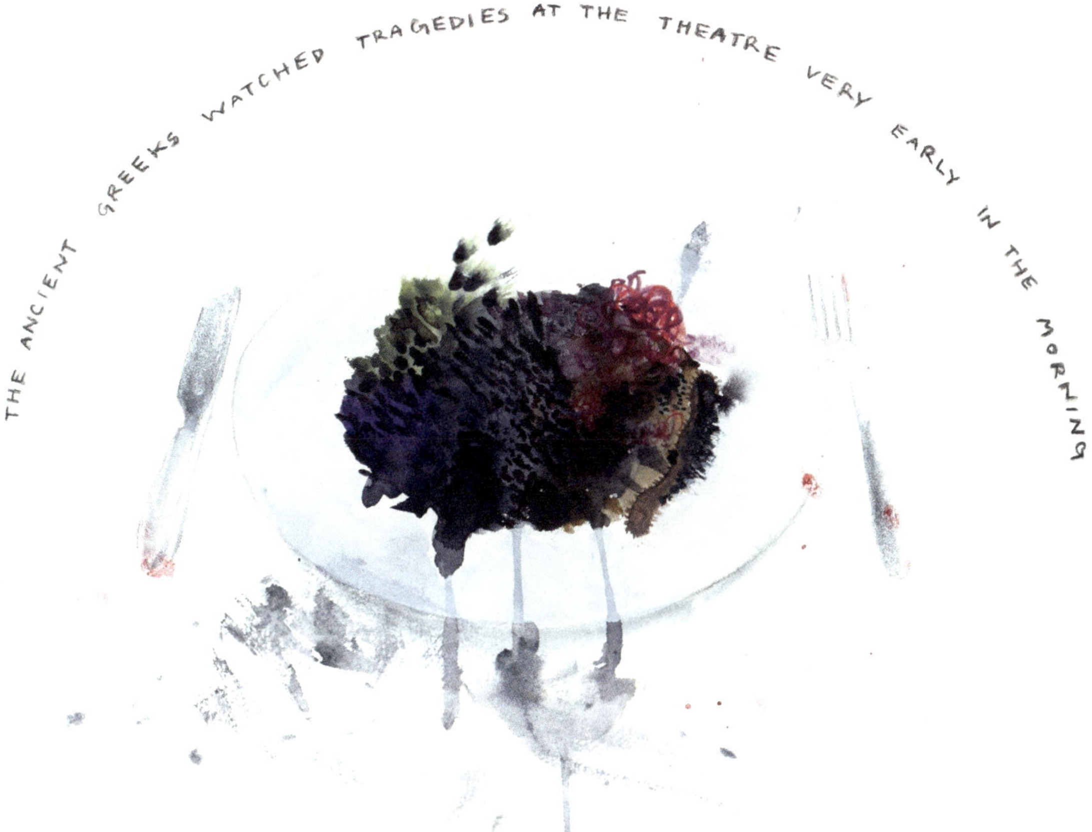

HELL FOR BREAKFAST

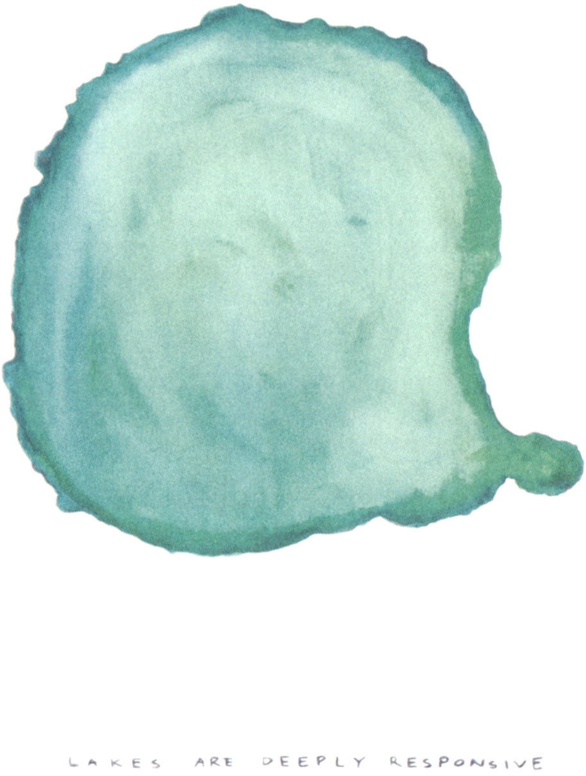

Lakes are Deeply Responsive

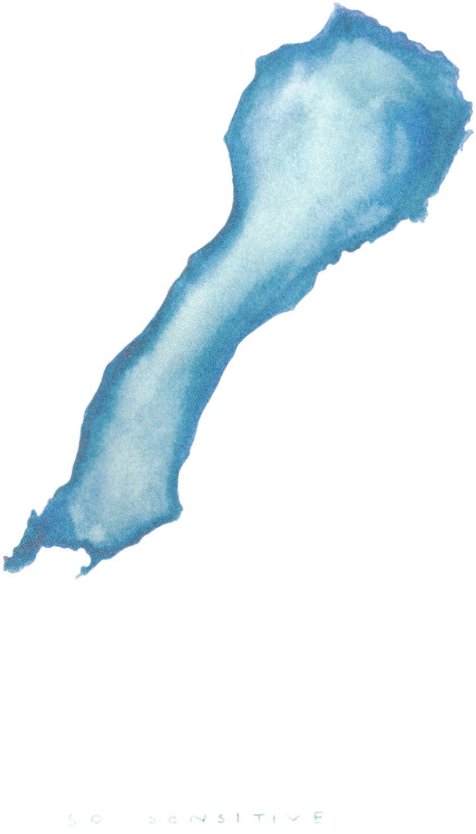

So Sensitive

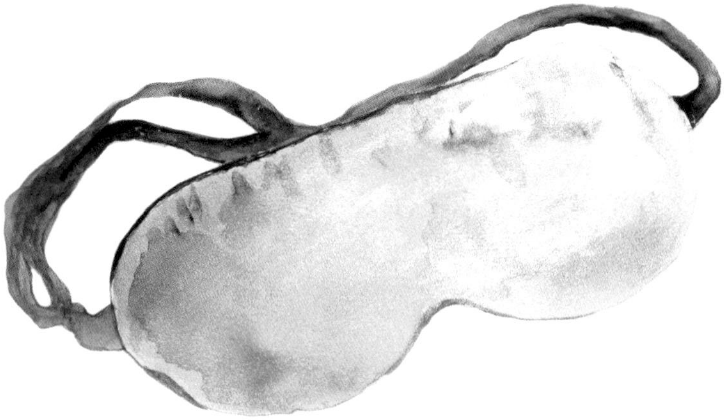

Sleep Mask

TO BE COMFORTABLE WITHOUT OUTLINE
DELICATELY VULGAR

Delicately Vulgar

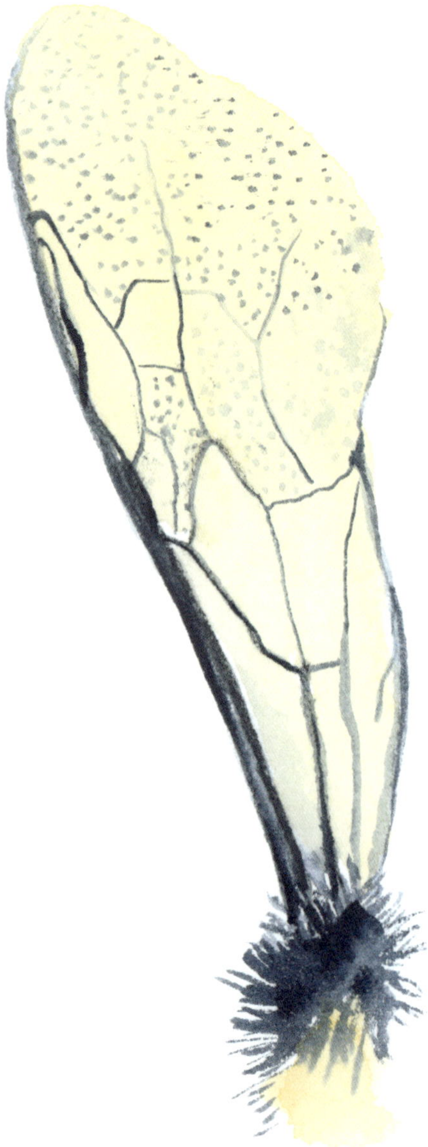

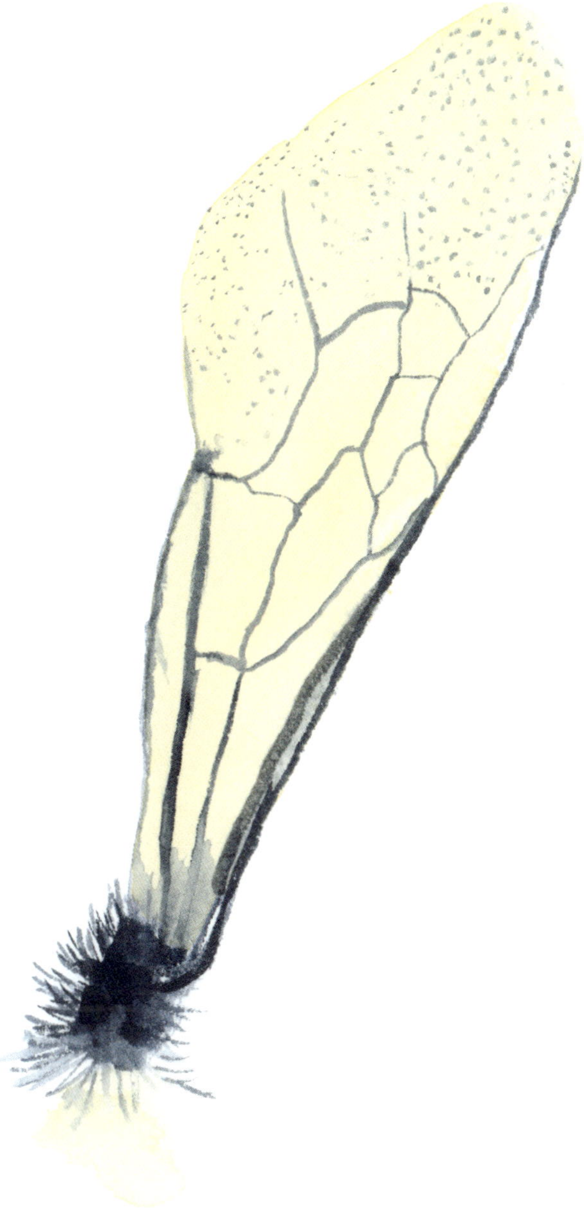

Bee Wings

Self-Portrait as Swiss Knife

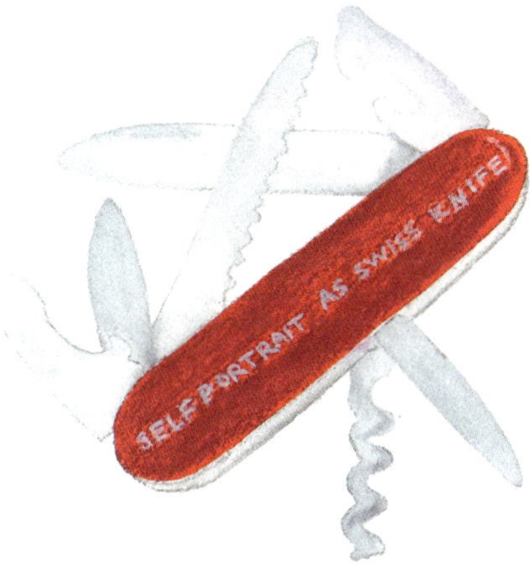
SELF PORTRAIT AS SWISS KNIFE

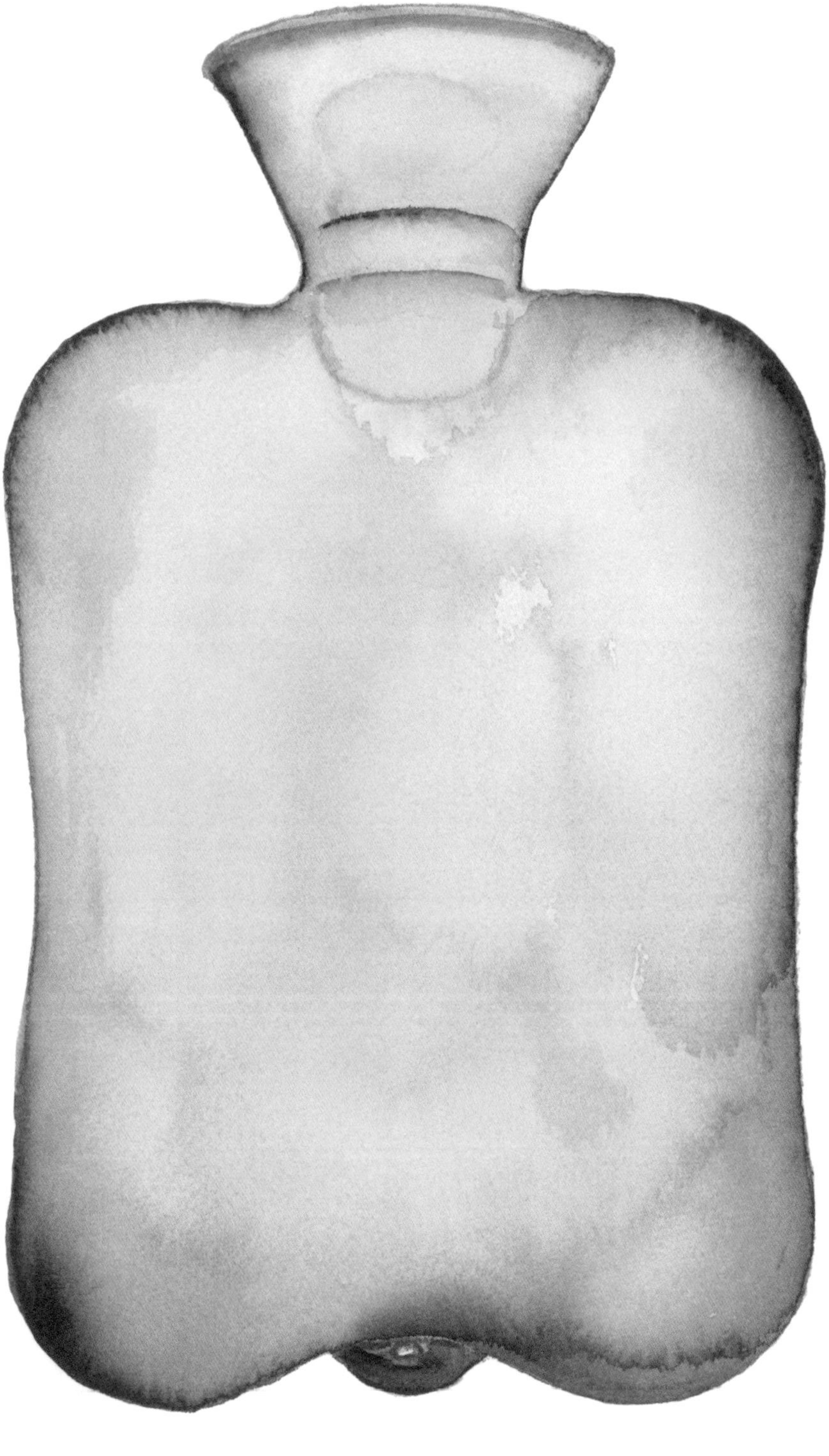

Hot Water Bottle

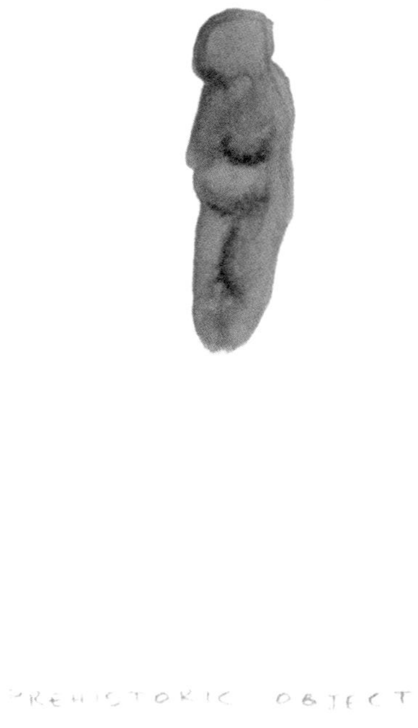

Prehistoric Object

Sexually Deceptive Pollination

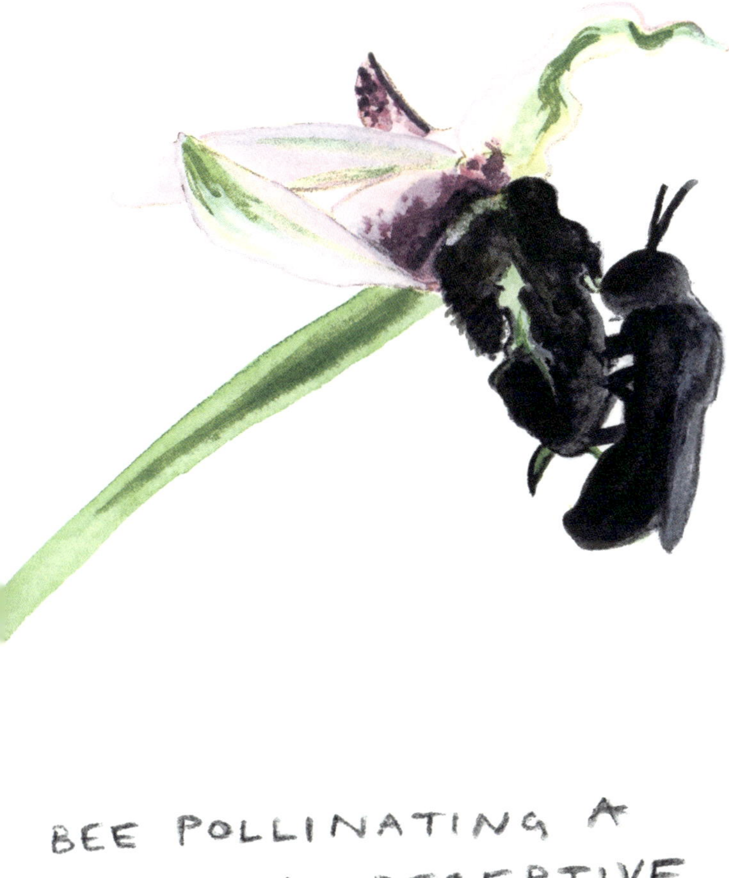

BEE POLLINATING A
SEXUALLY DECEPTIVE
ORCHID (OPHRYS APIFERA)

Self-Portrait as Espresso Pot

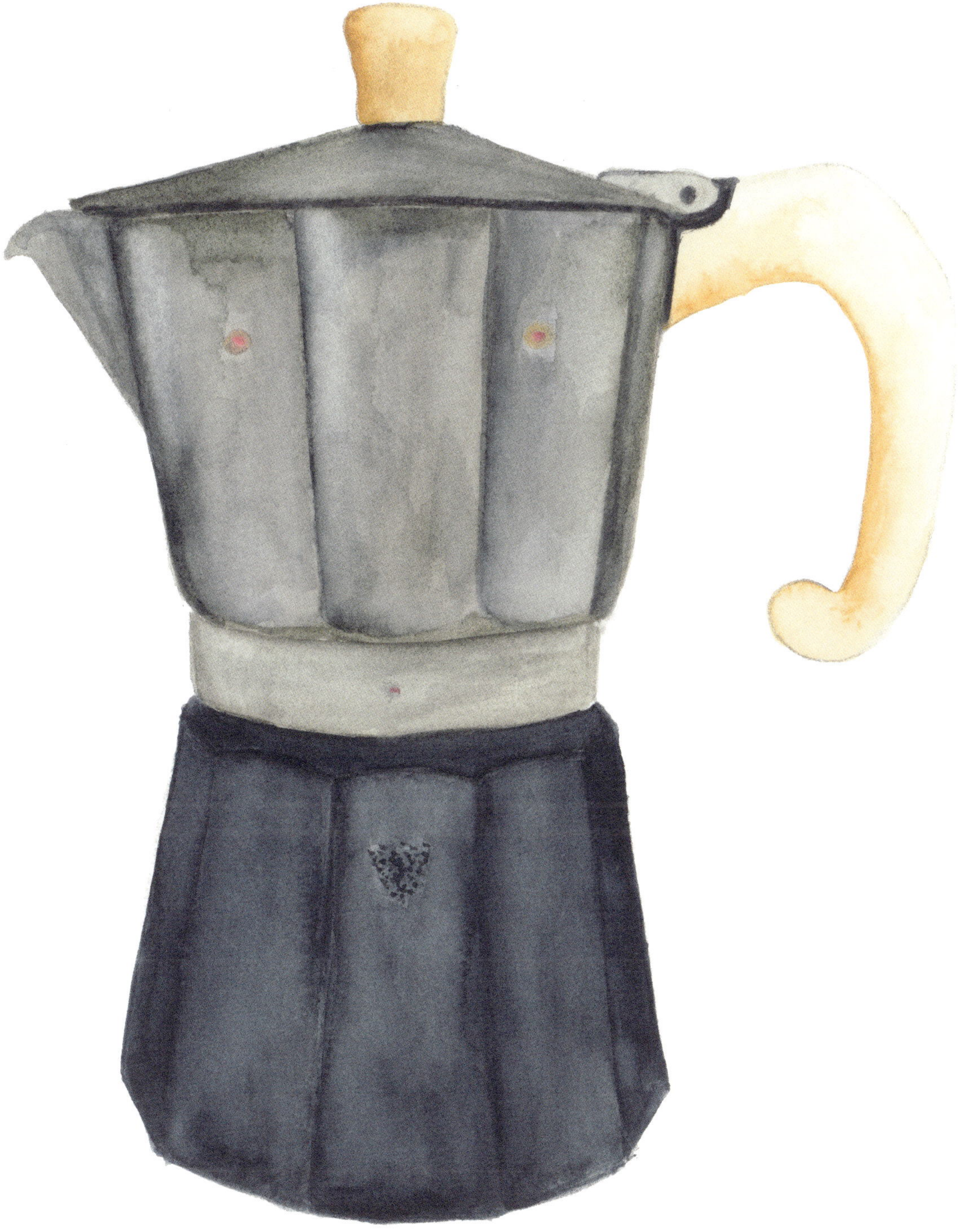

ROUTINE SURPISE

Routine "Surpise"

R

Missing R

Imaginary Scenario

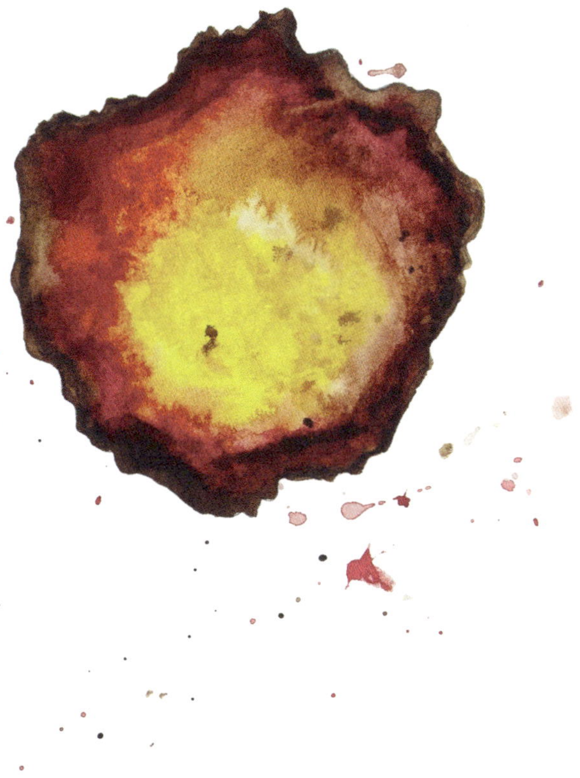

IMAGINARY SCENARIO

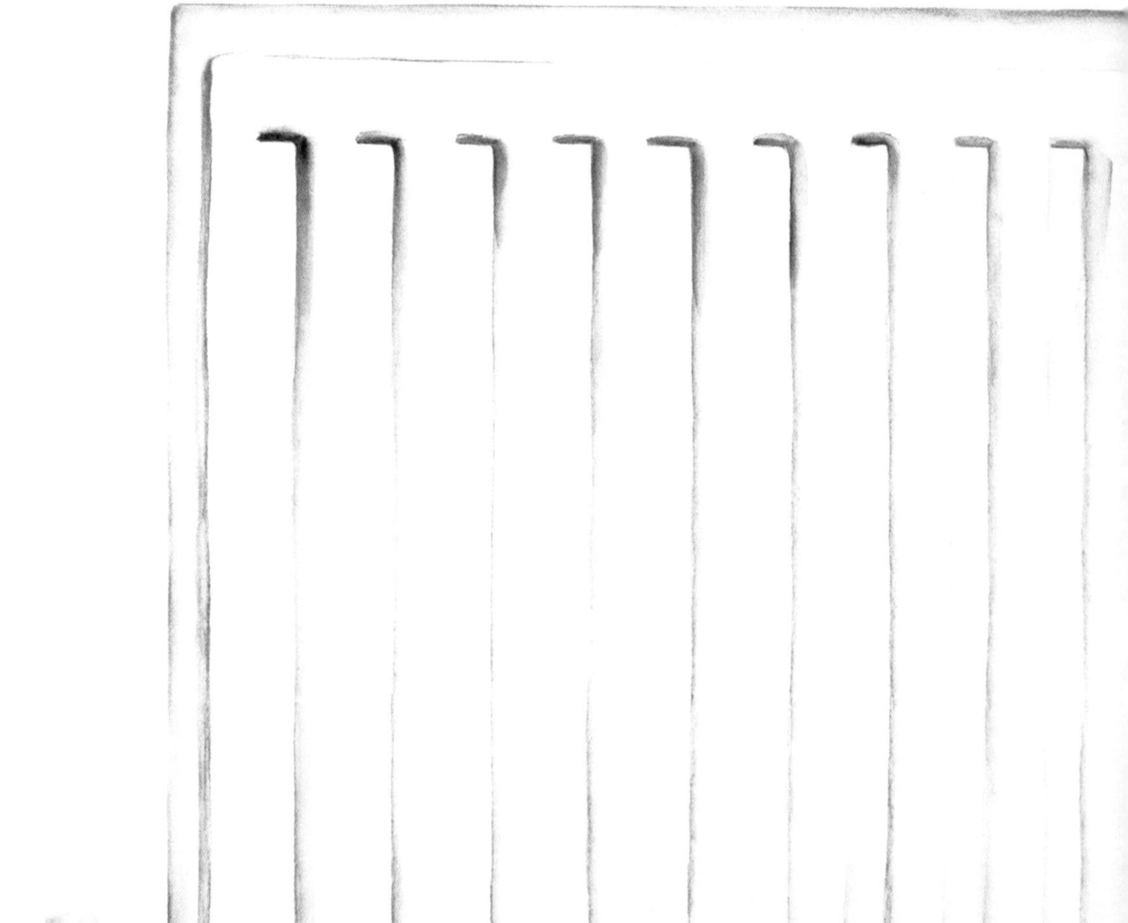

Radiator

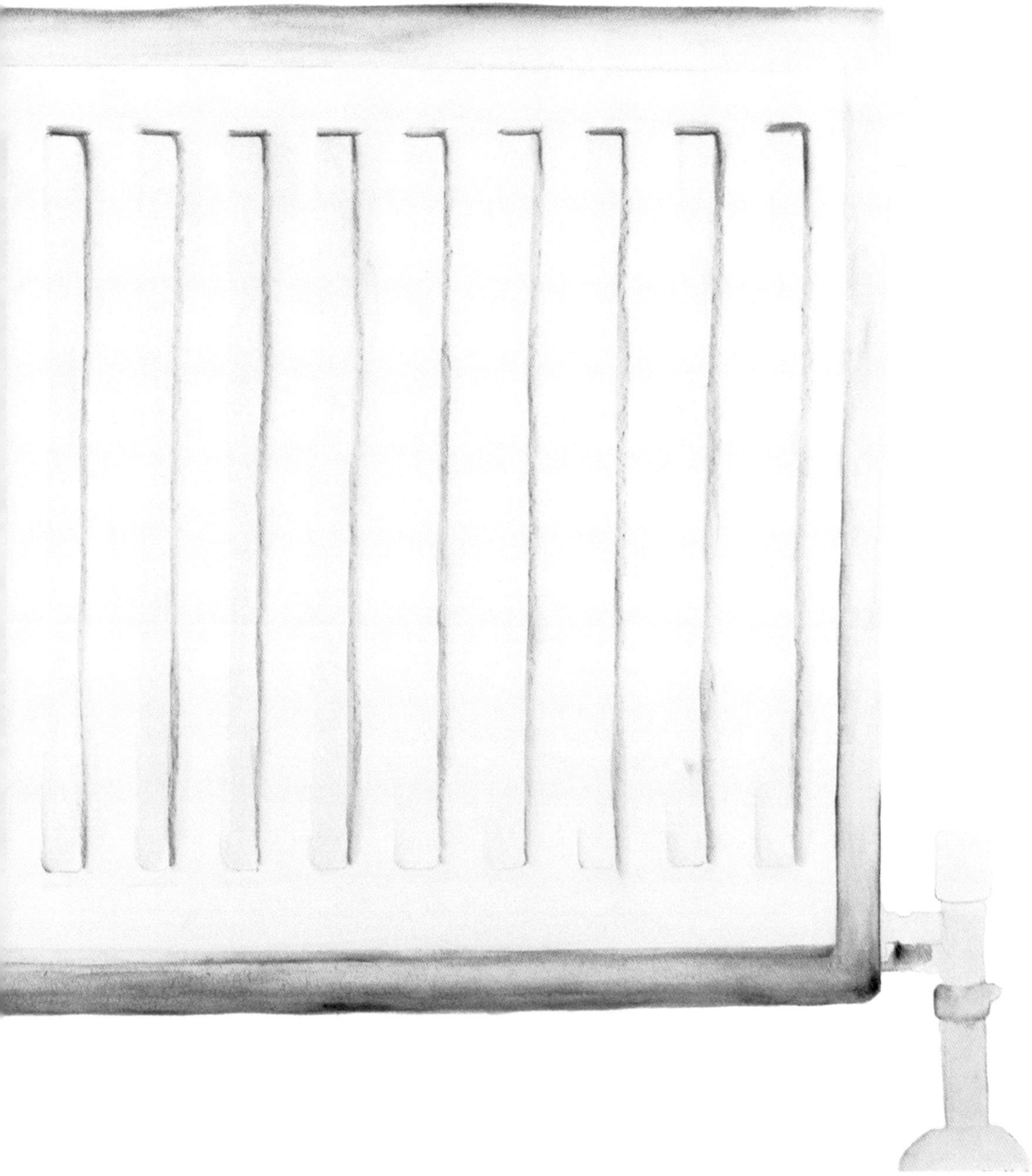

Work Only in Centimeters

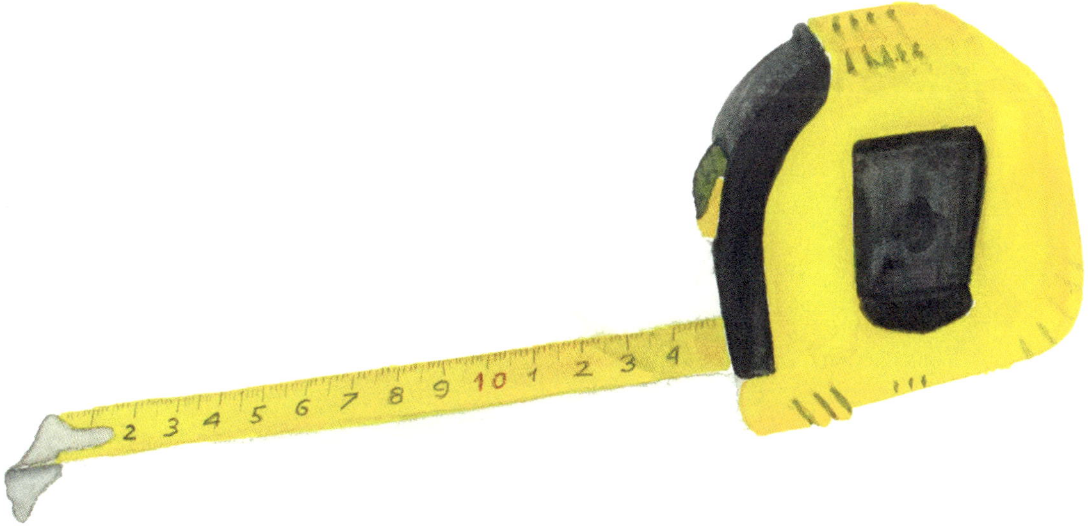
2 3 4 5 6 7 8 9 10 1 2 3 4

Swimming with Piglet

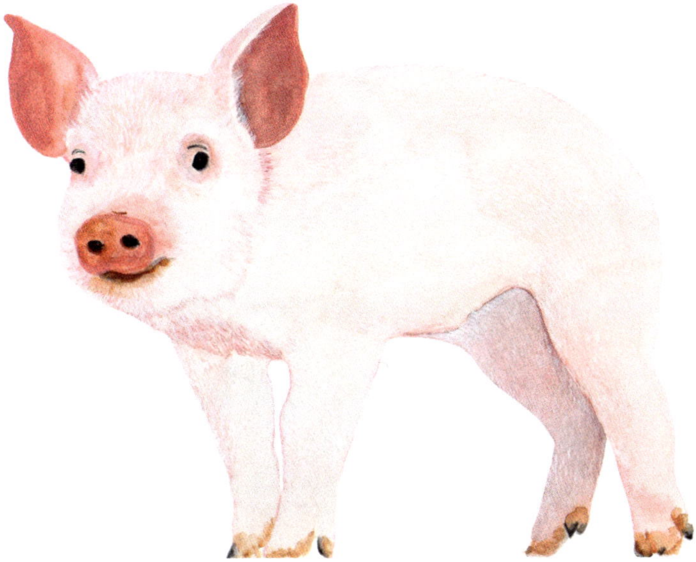

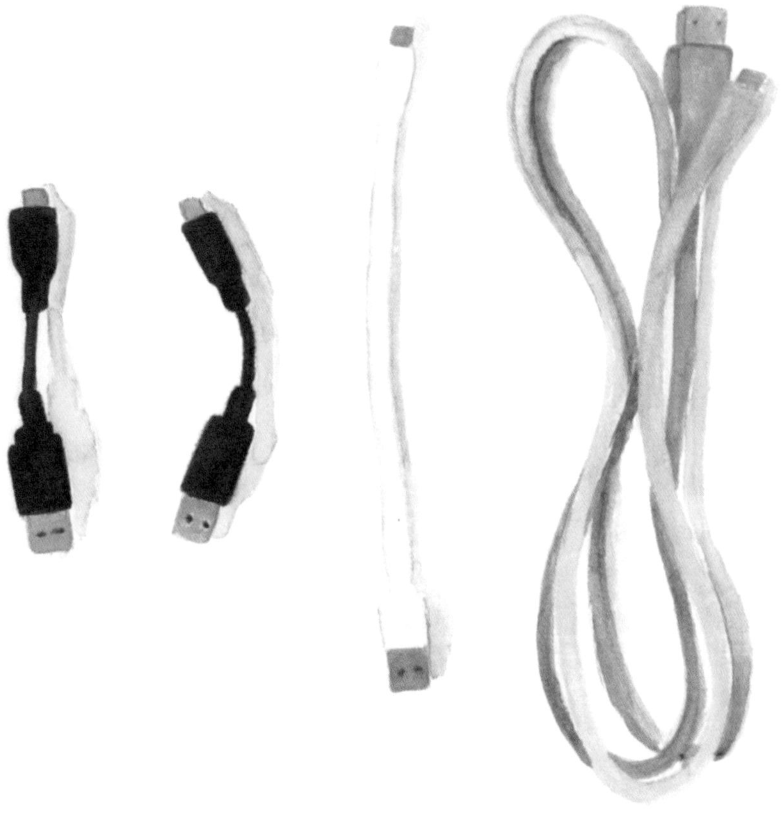

Cords

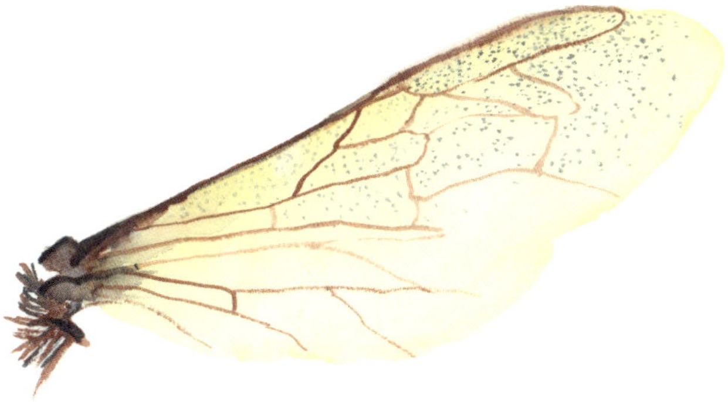

Bee Wing

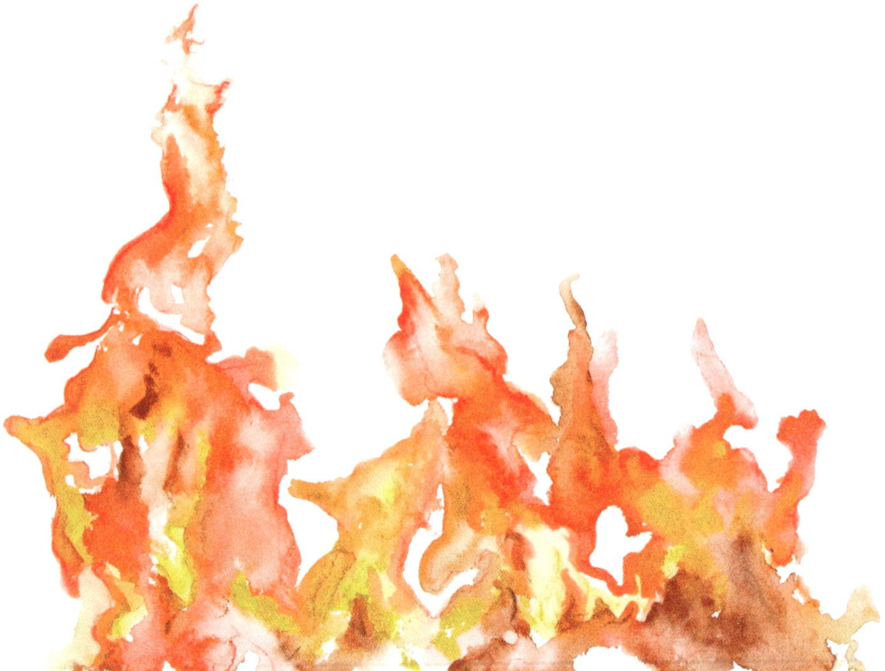

Watercolor Fire

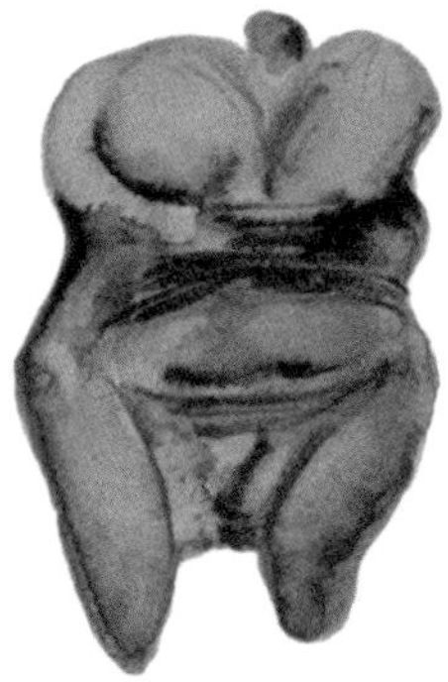

Prehistoric

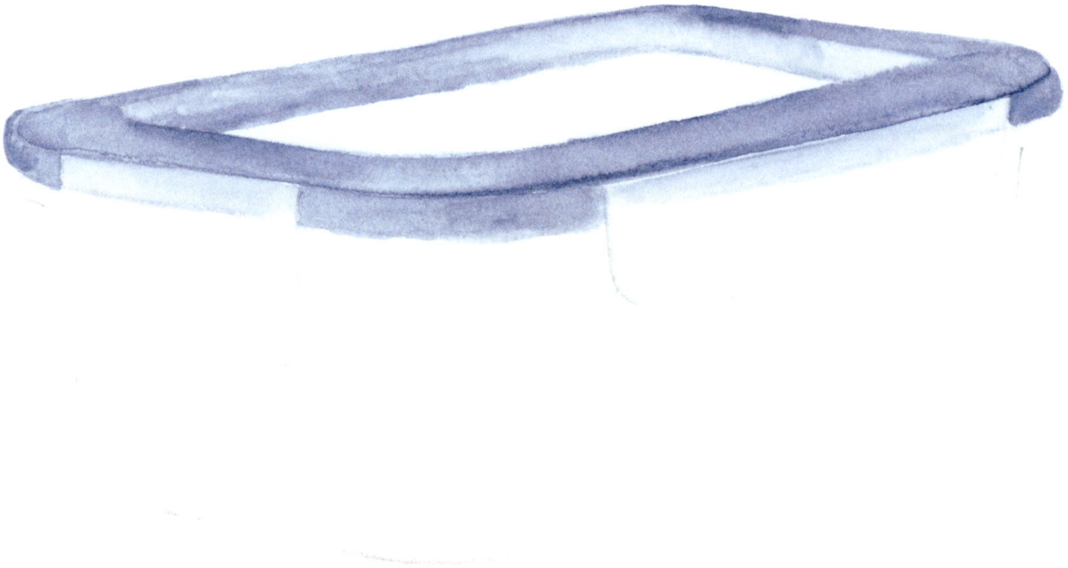

Tupperware

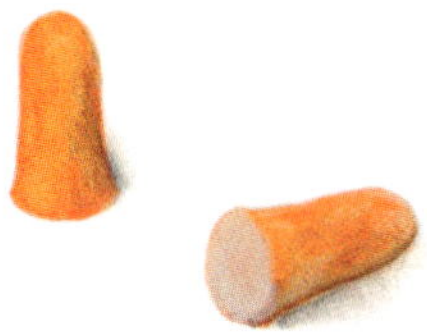

Earplugs

Squirrel

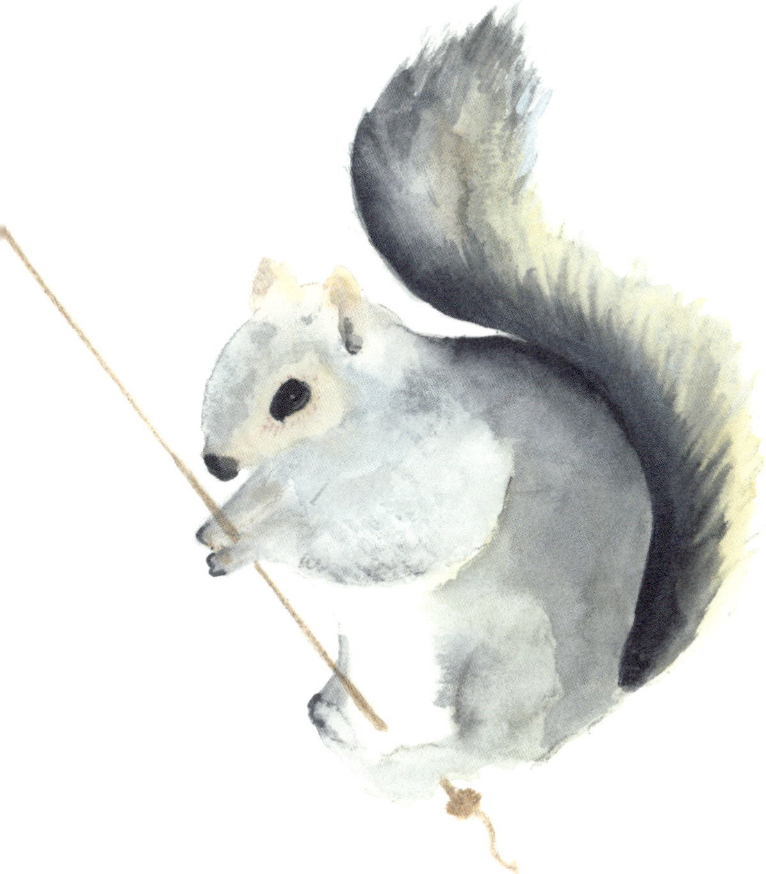

Hybridchildren

HYBRIDCHILDREN

Self-Portrait as Blender

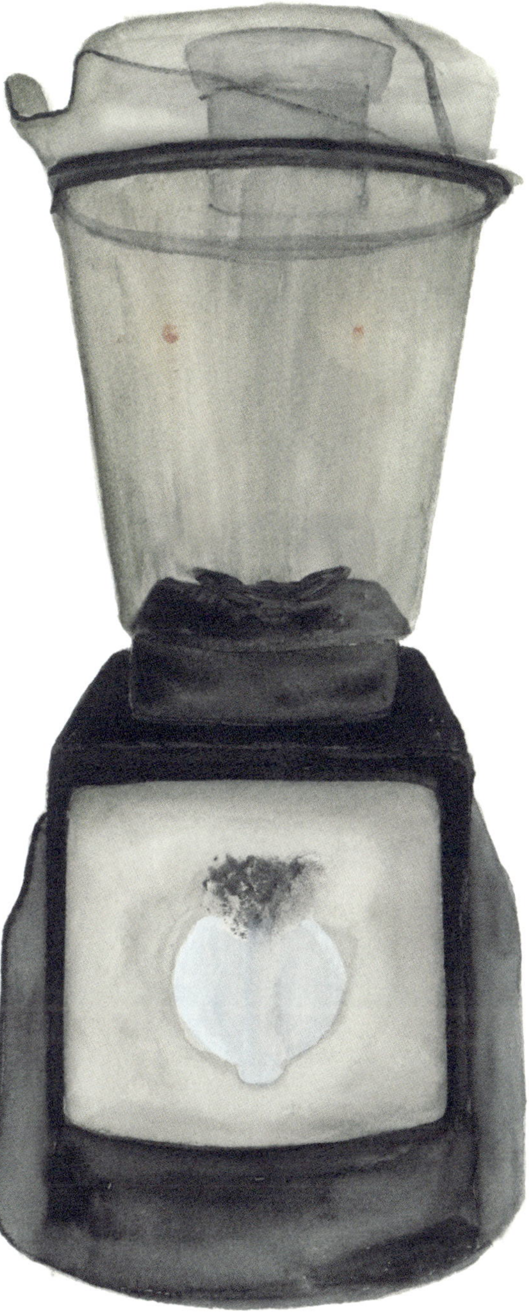

SELF PORTRAIT AS BLENDER

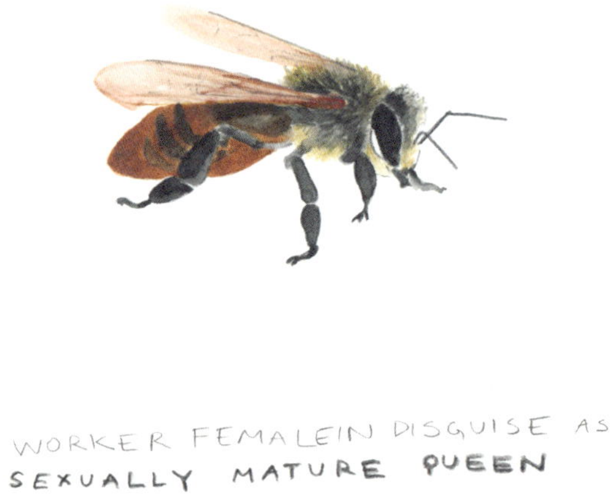

Worker Female in Disguise as Sexually Mature Queen

Parasol Mushroom

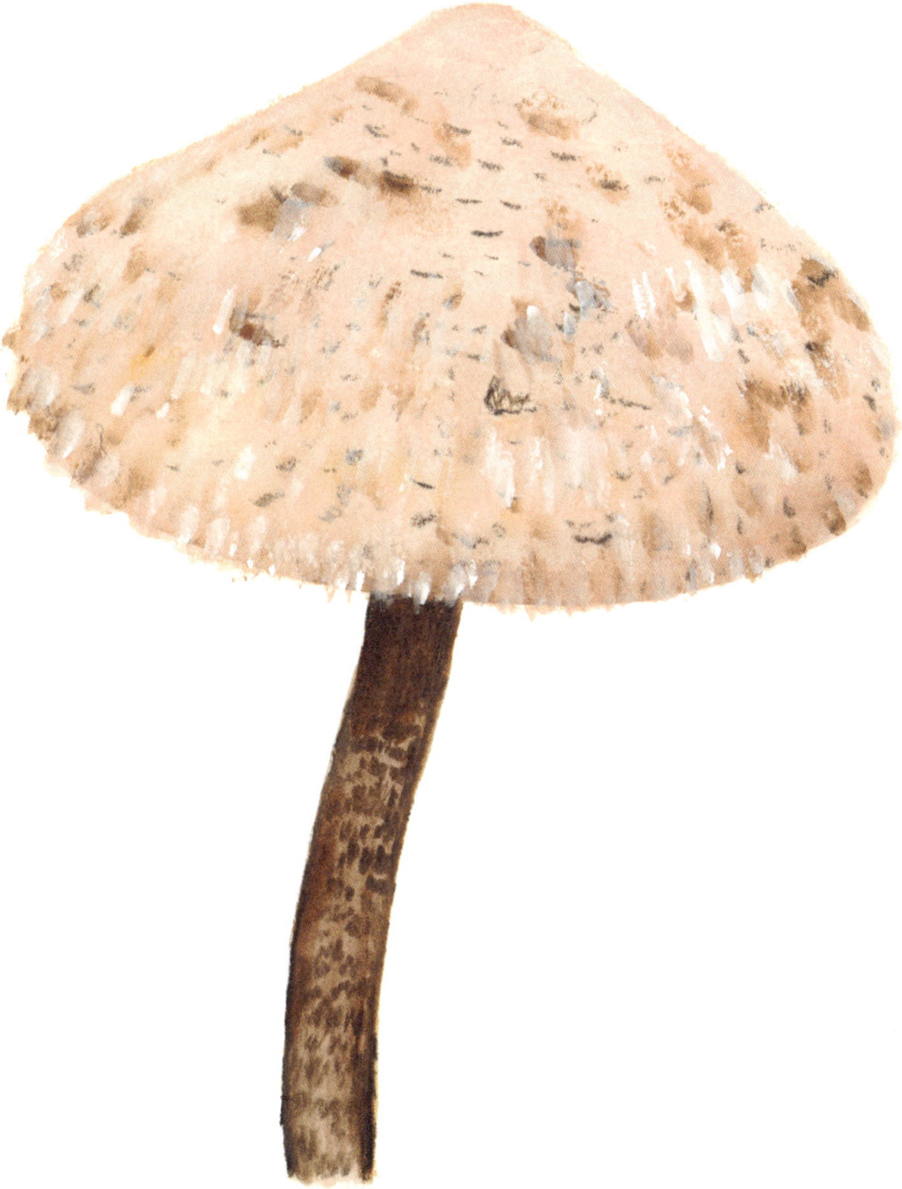

Earth is Top-Heavy

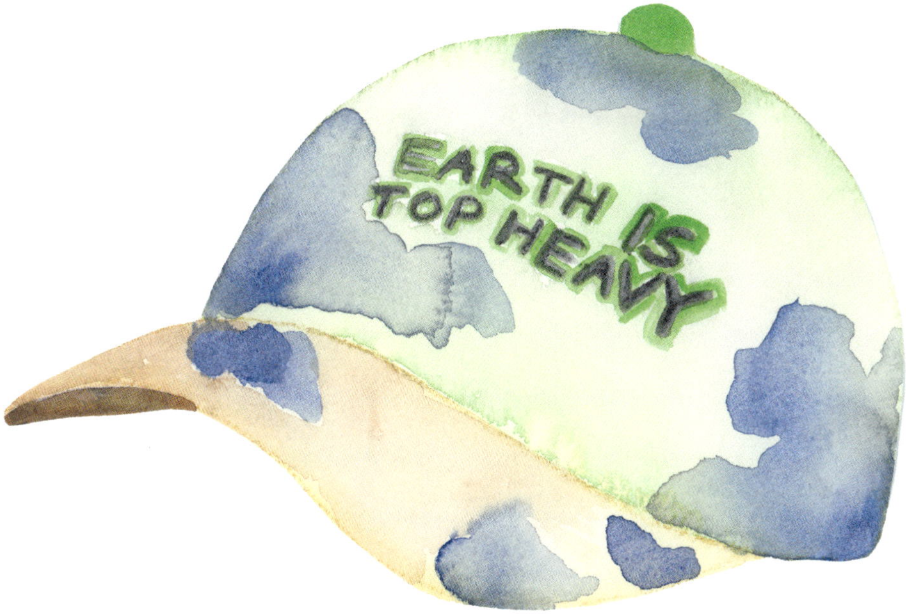
EARTH IS
TOP HEAVY

Kelp Eating Sheep

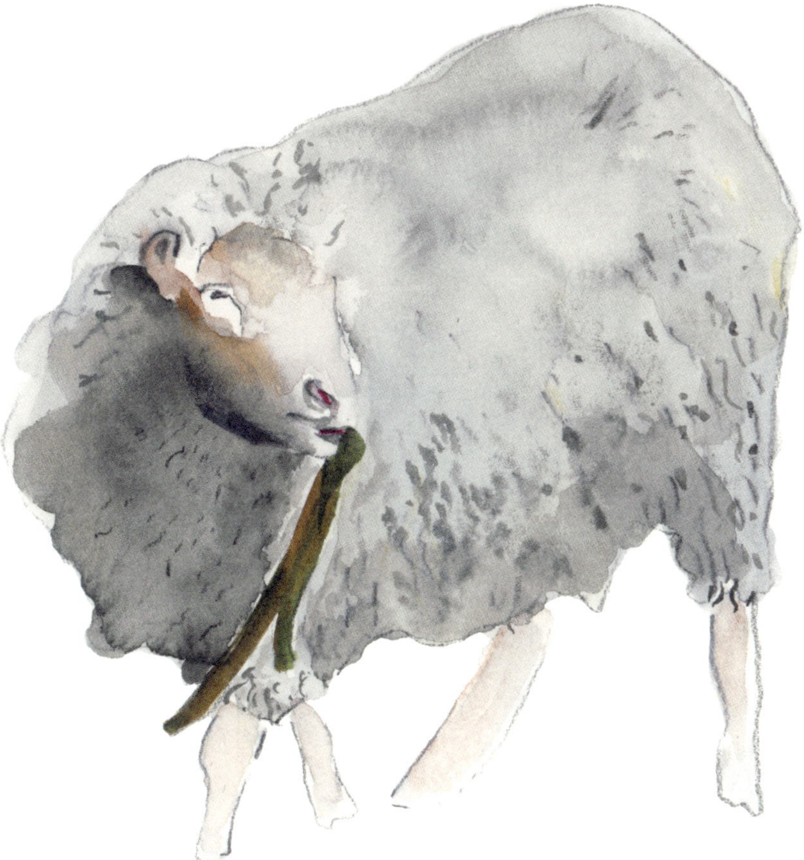

KELP EATING SHEEP

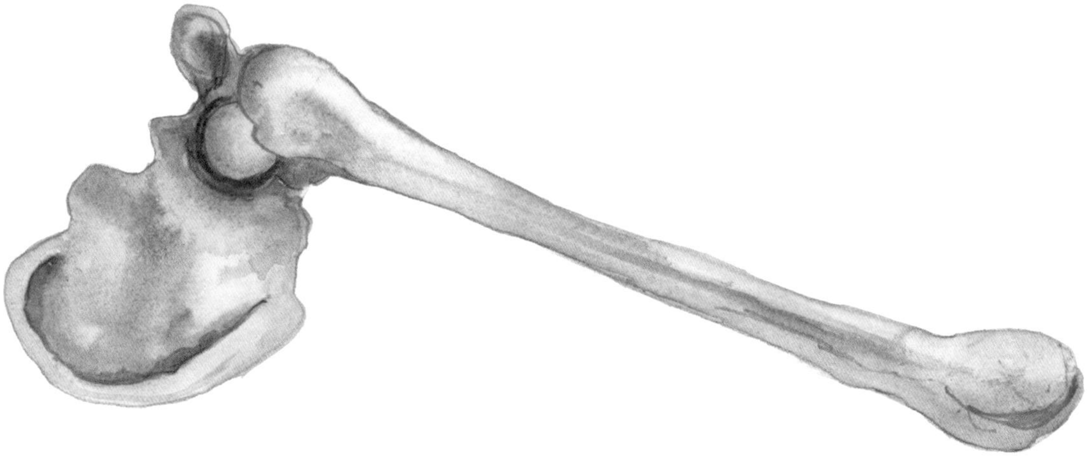

Hip Fidget

The Beekeeper (After Bruegel)

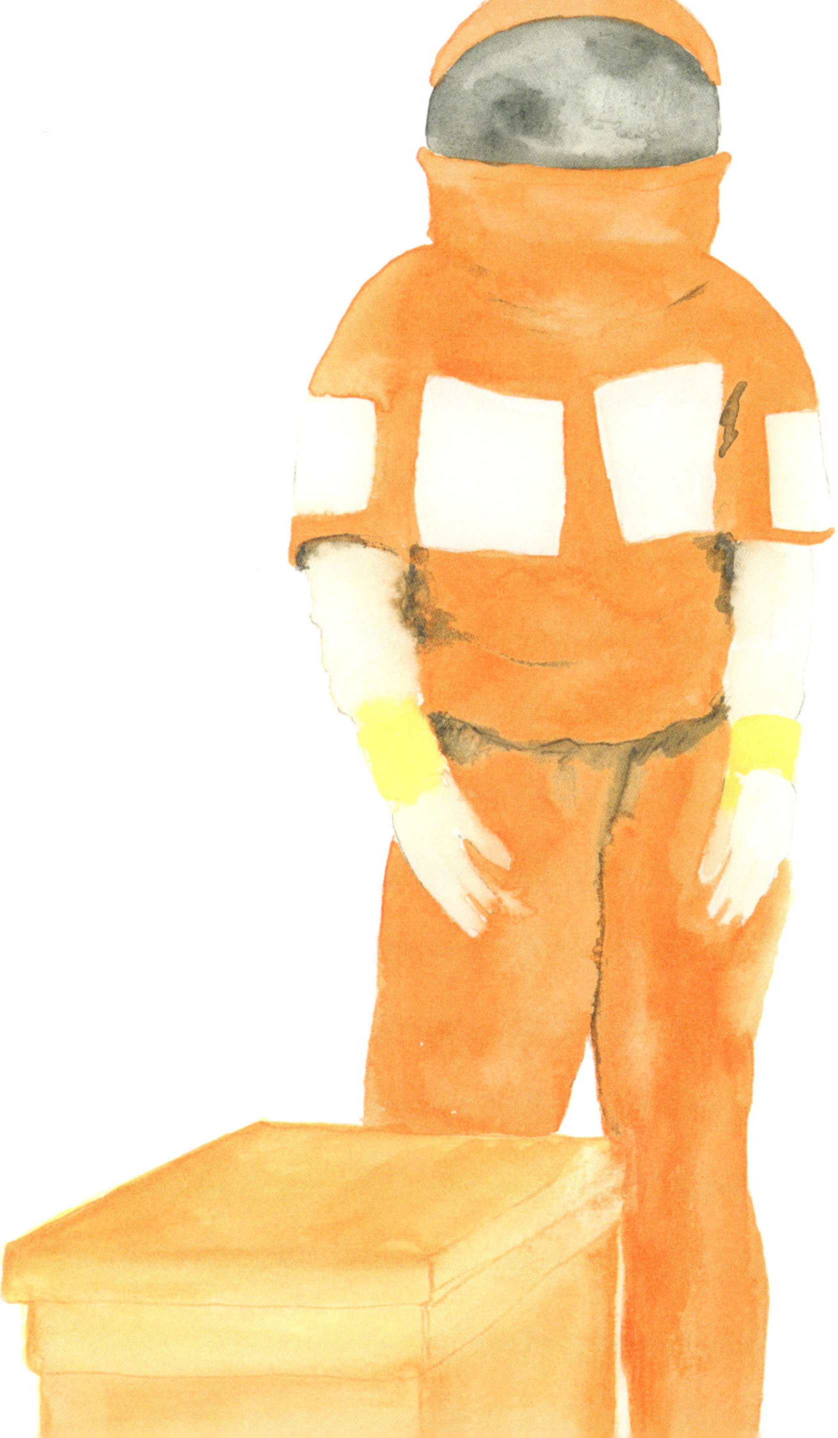

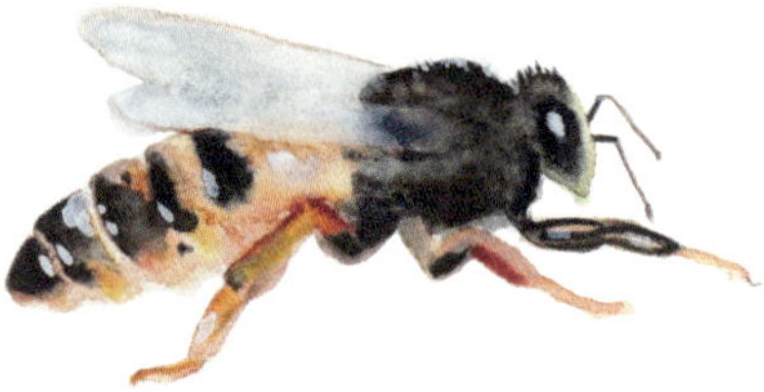

Sexually Mature Queen

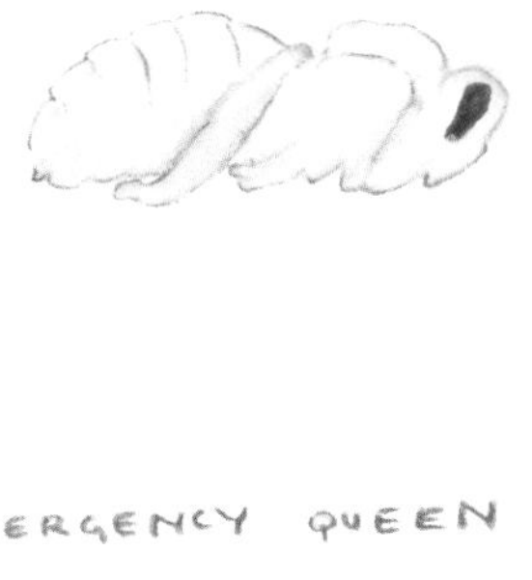

Emergency Queen

Torrential Rain

Burn Sadness Like Calories

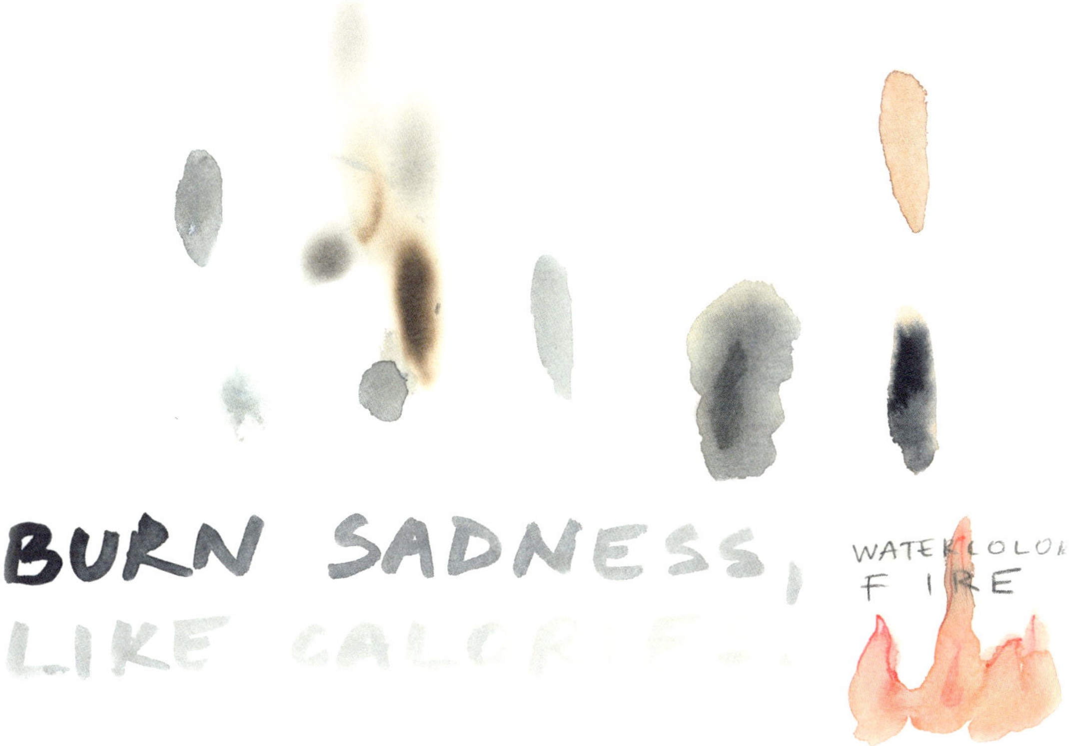
BURN SADNESS,
LIKE COLOR F...
WATERCOLOR
FIRE

Something Good for Nervous System

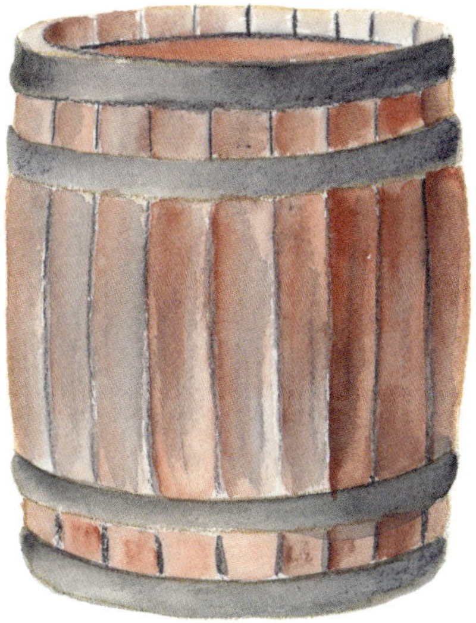
MARINATING

Moon Moving Away

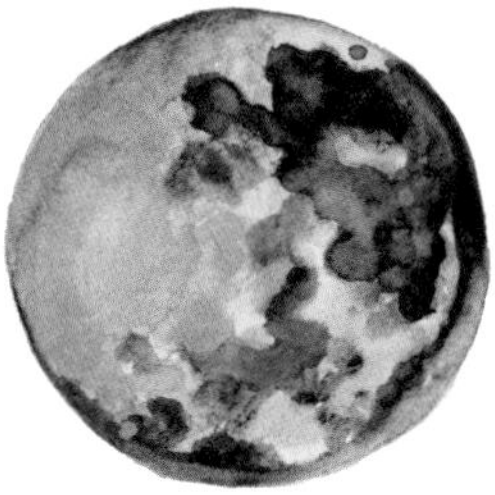

THE MOON IS SLOWLY MOVING AWAY FROM EARTH,
AT THE SPEED OF OUR FINGERNAILS GROWING.

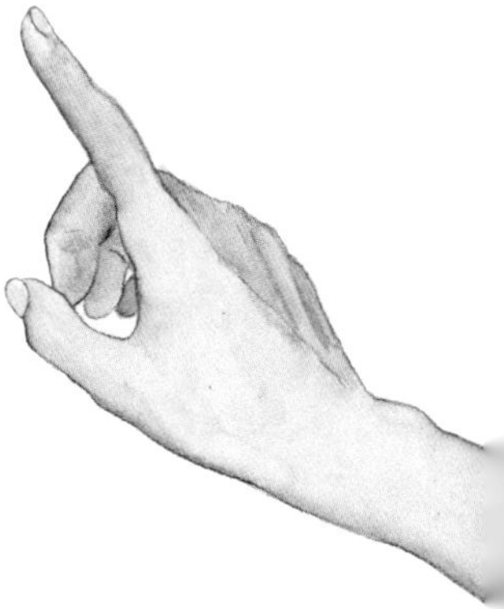

Mud Slides

Orange Slippers

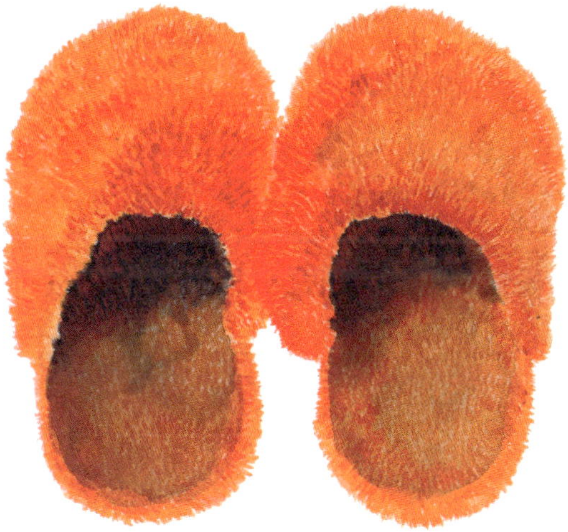

Pillow (After Dürer)

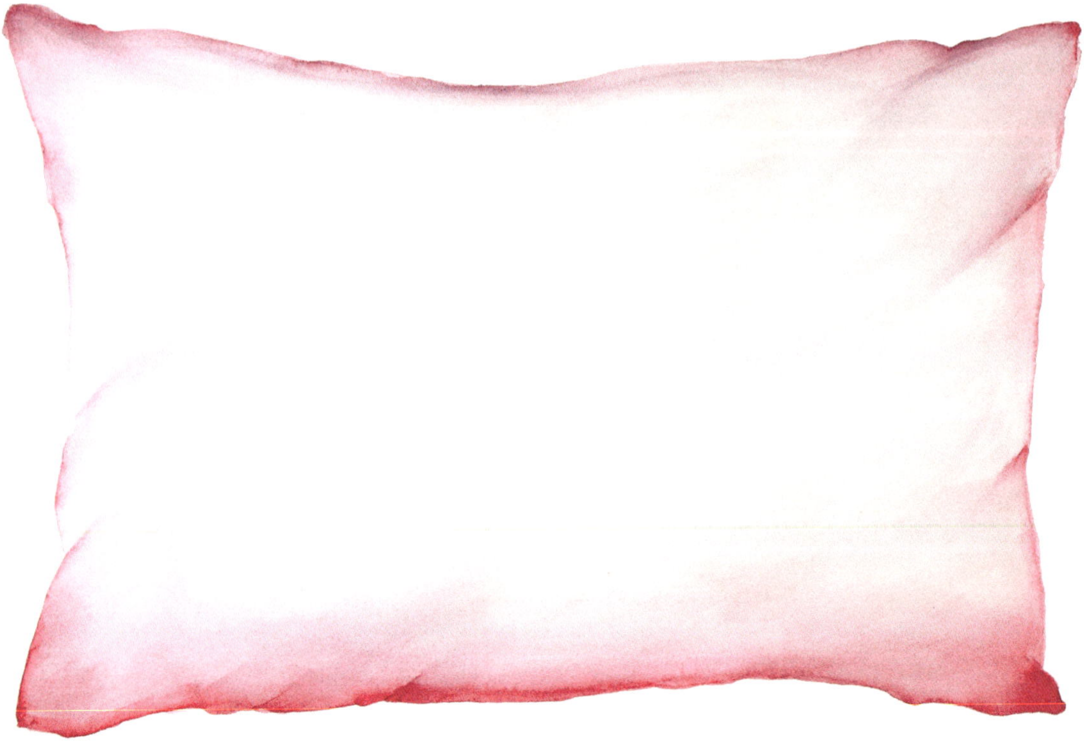

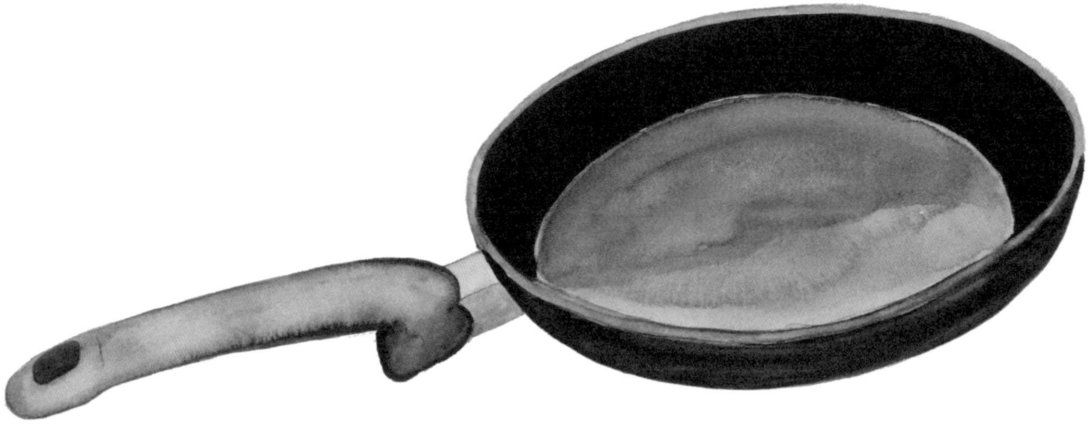

Frying Pan

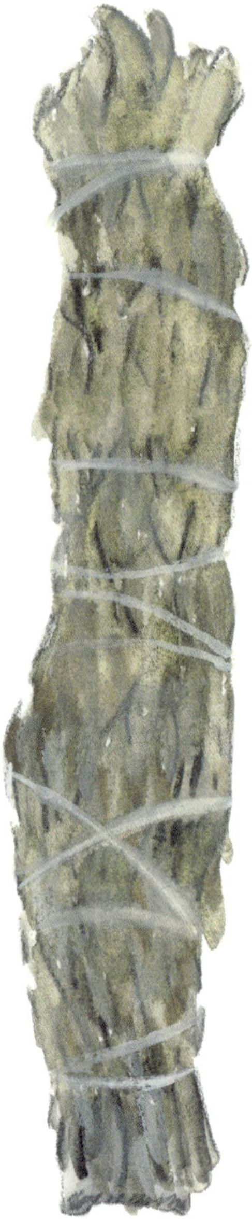

Sage

Bunny Ears

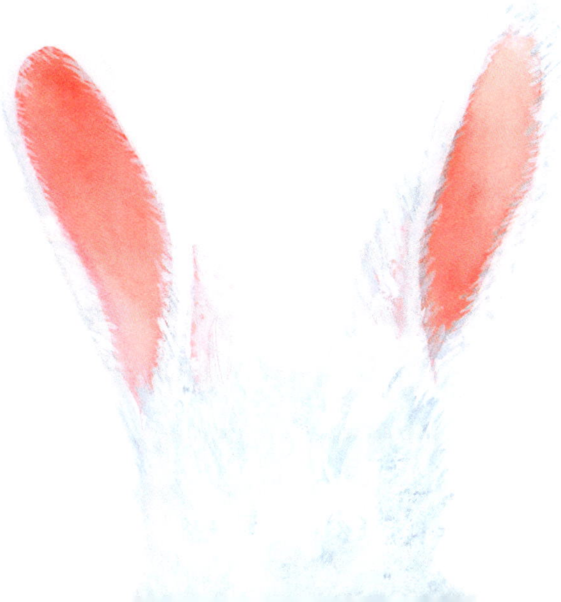

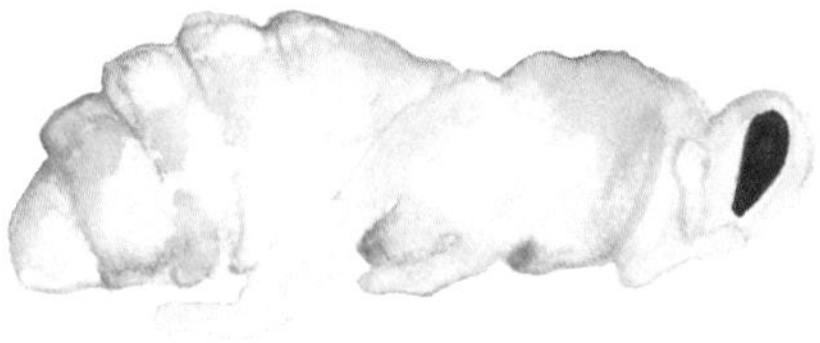

Emergency Queen

Pillow (After Dürer)

Spine

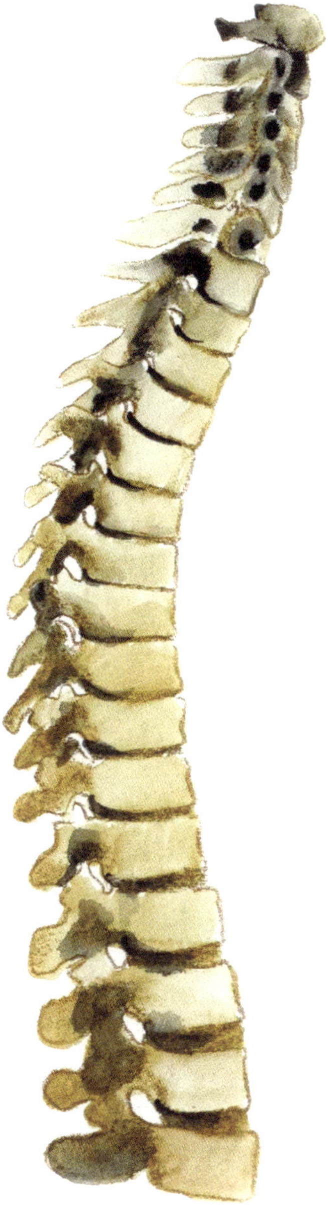

Prawn

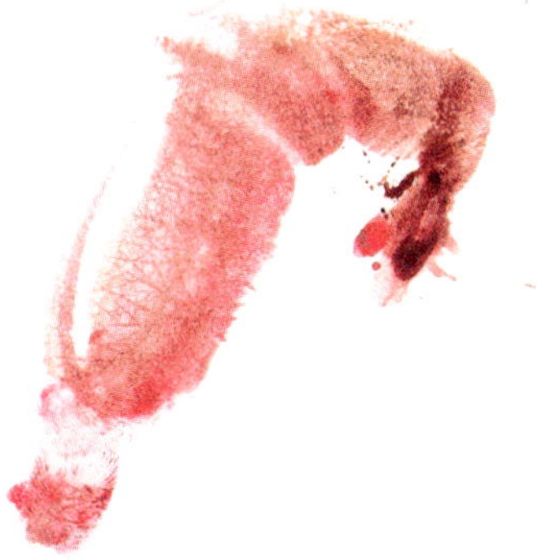

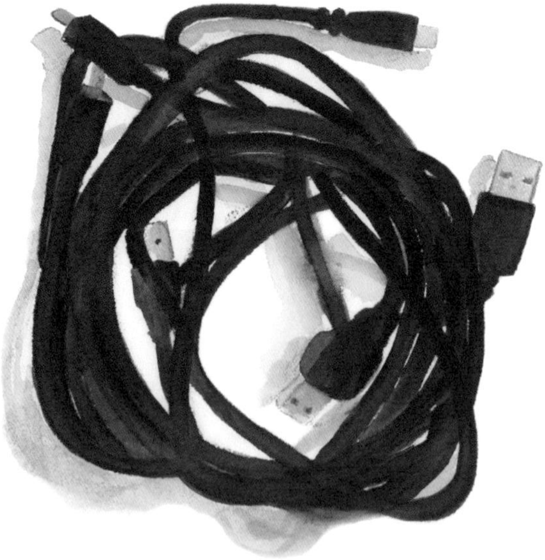

Cords

House Cat

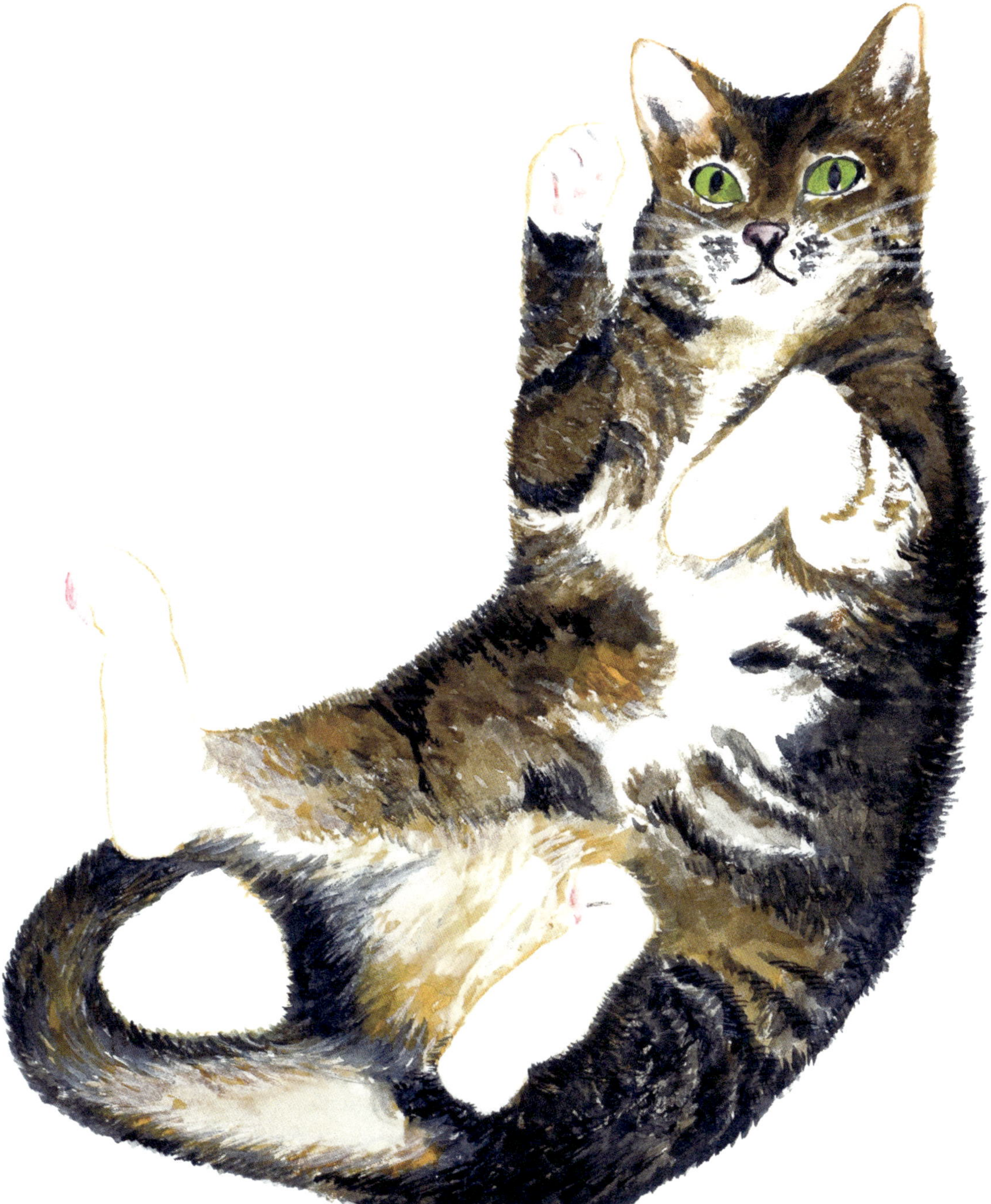

Self-Portrait as Pepper Grinder

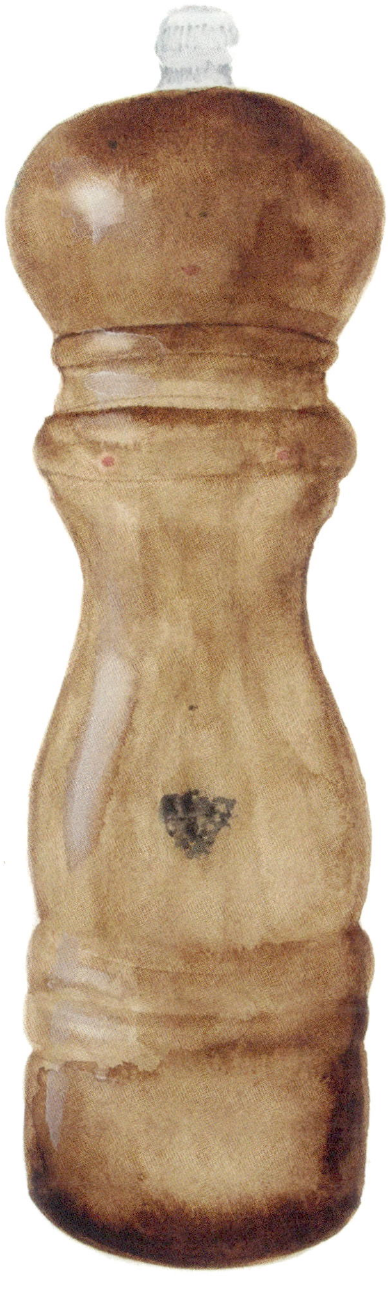

Honey Laundering

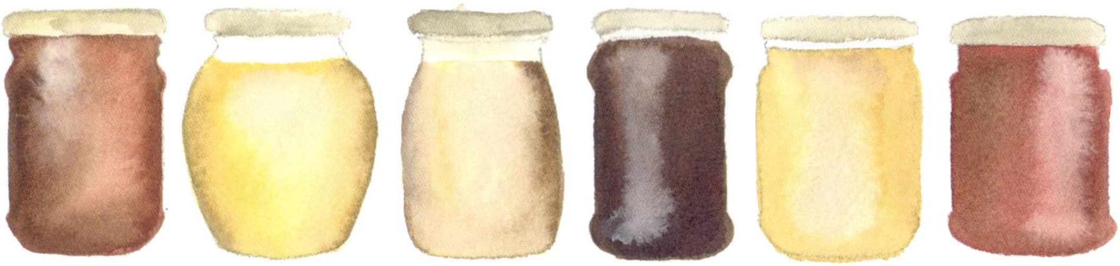

HONEY LAUNDERING

Some Flowers Require Vibration

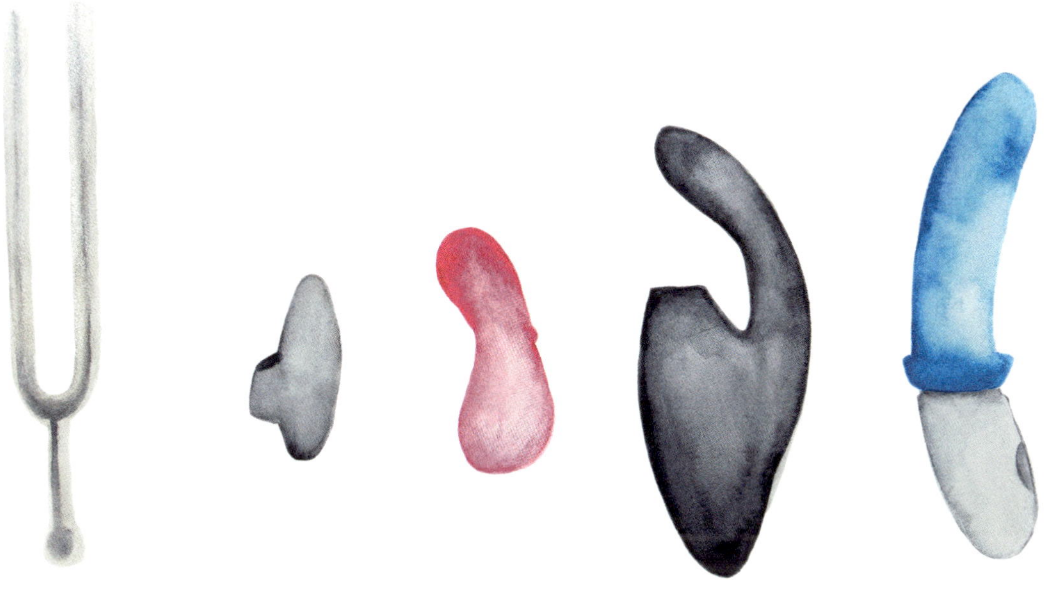

Levity Rocks

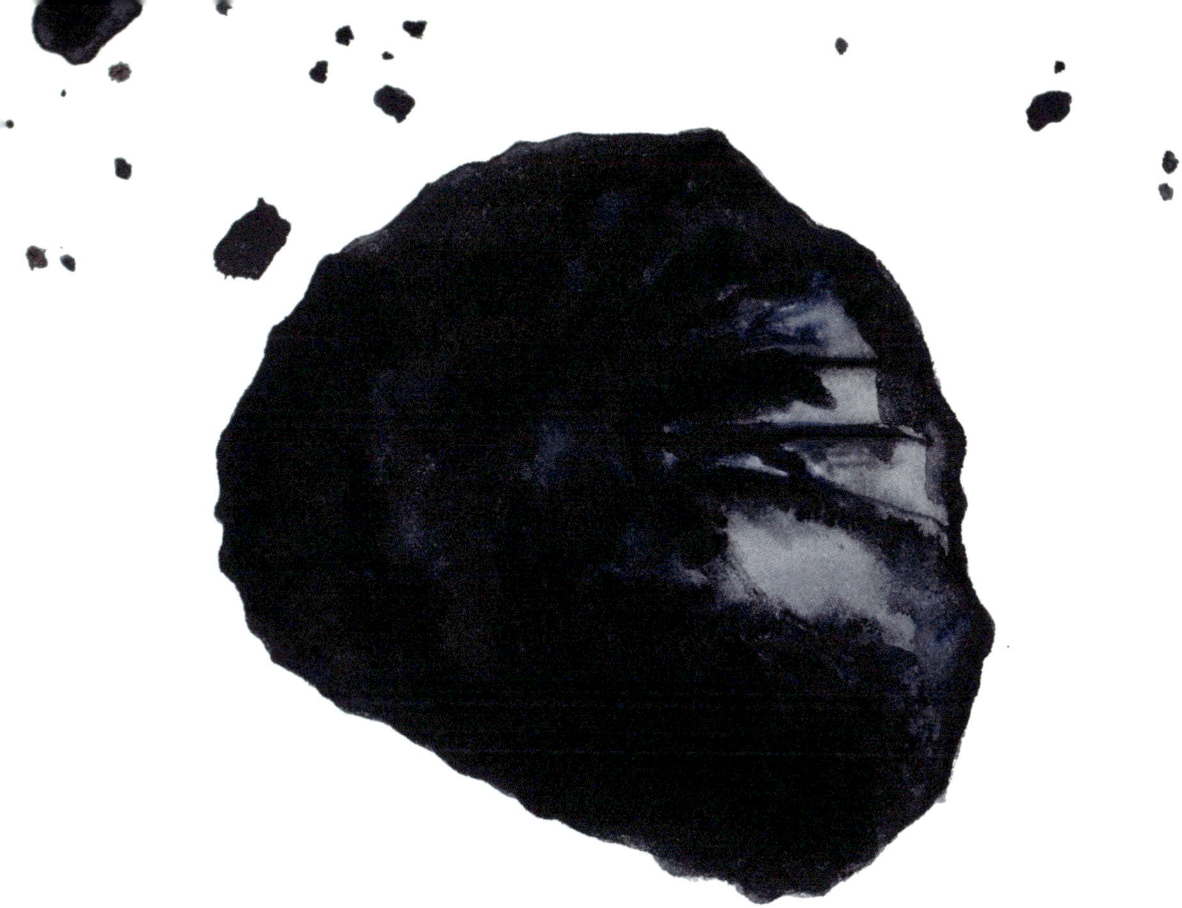

LEVITY ROCKS

Languishing

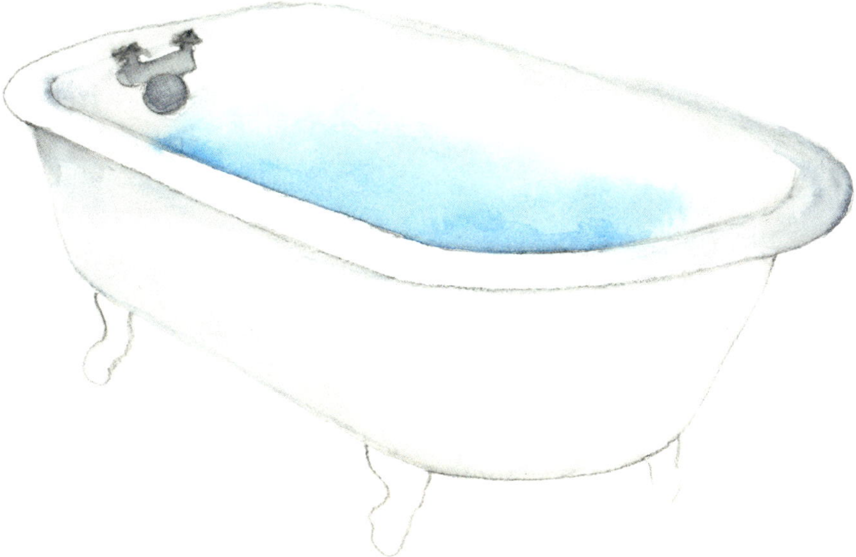

LANGUISHING

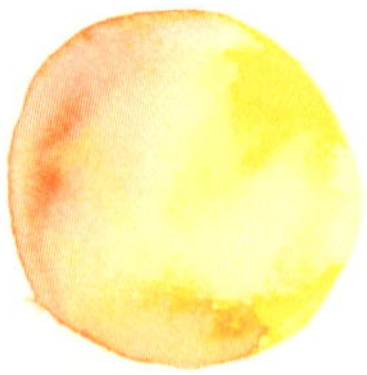

Egg

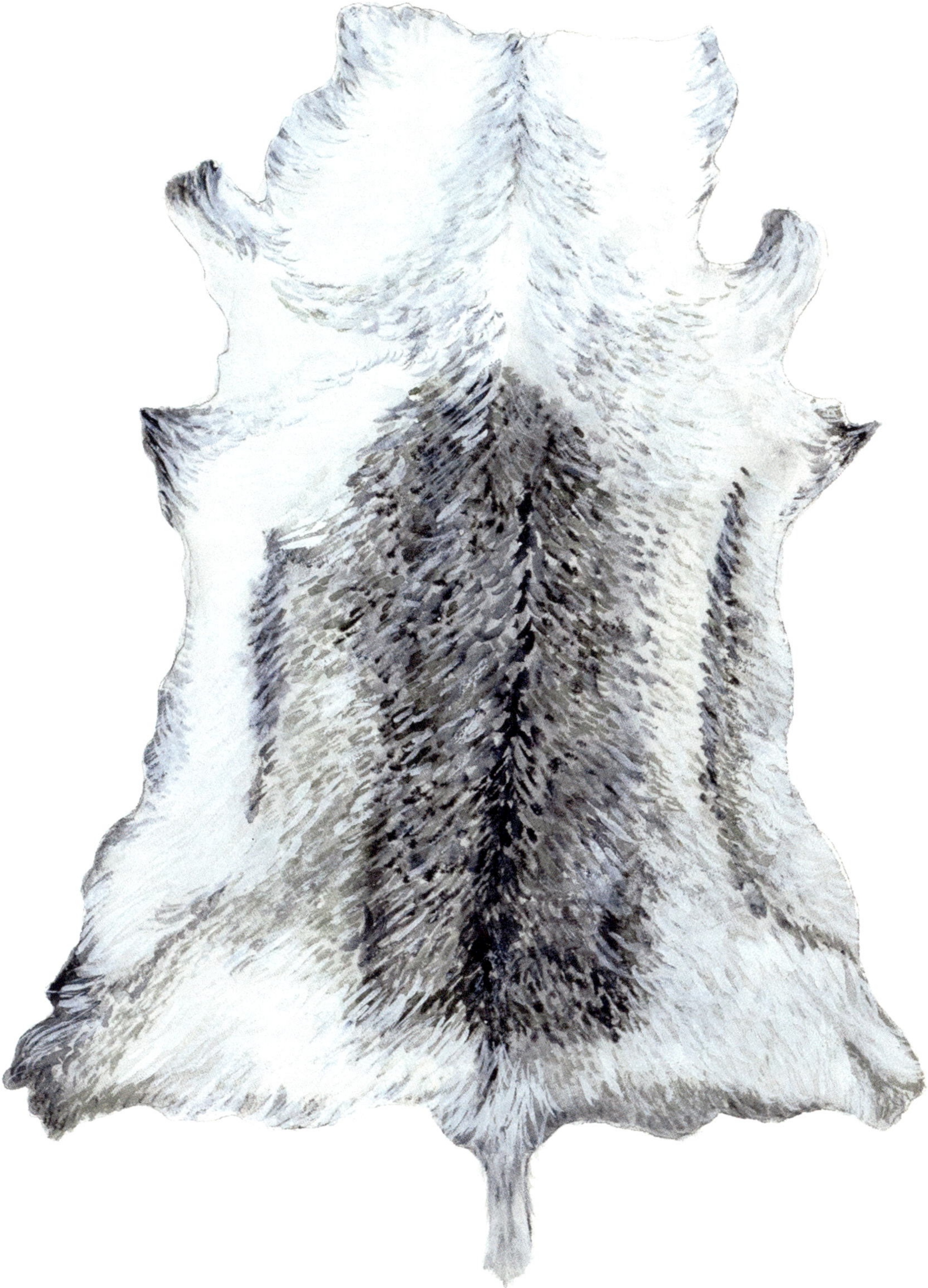

Sheep Skin

Early Hygiene Care

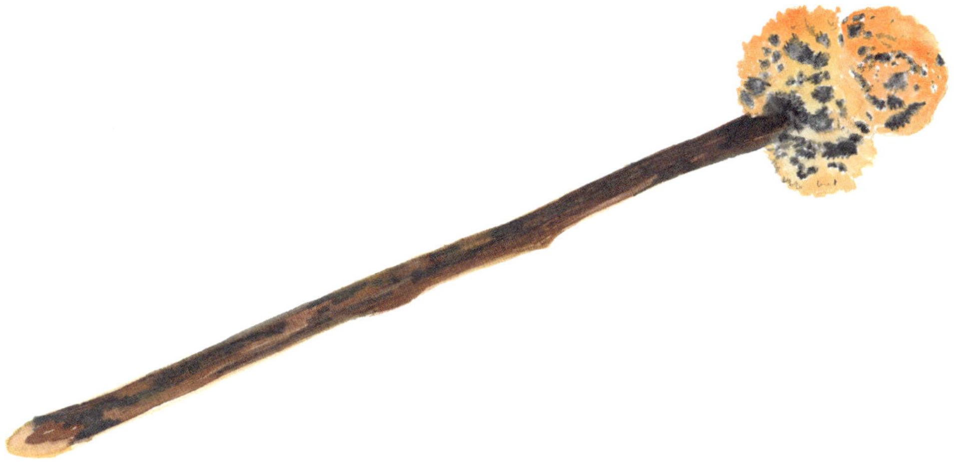

XYLOSPONGIUM
(SPONGE ON A STICK)
EARLY HYGIENIC CARE

Soup

IF YOU COMBINE SUN, WATER AND WIND, YOU GET A KIND OF SOUP

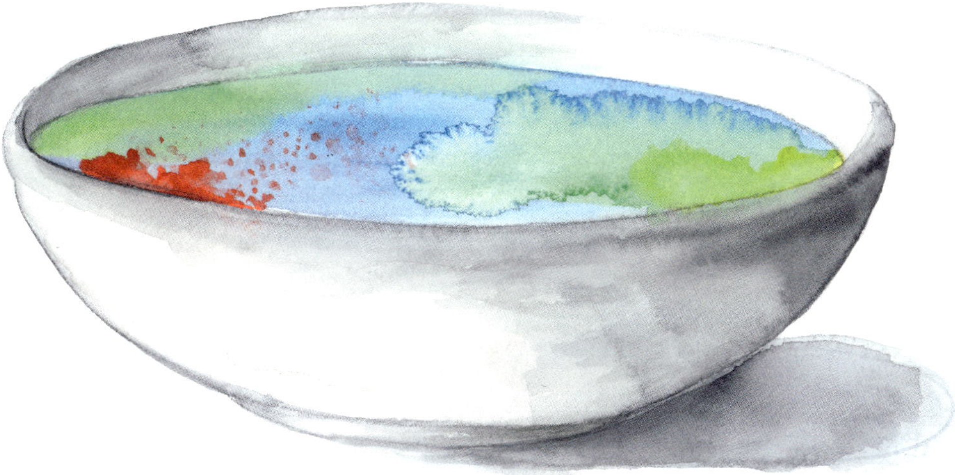

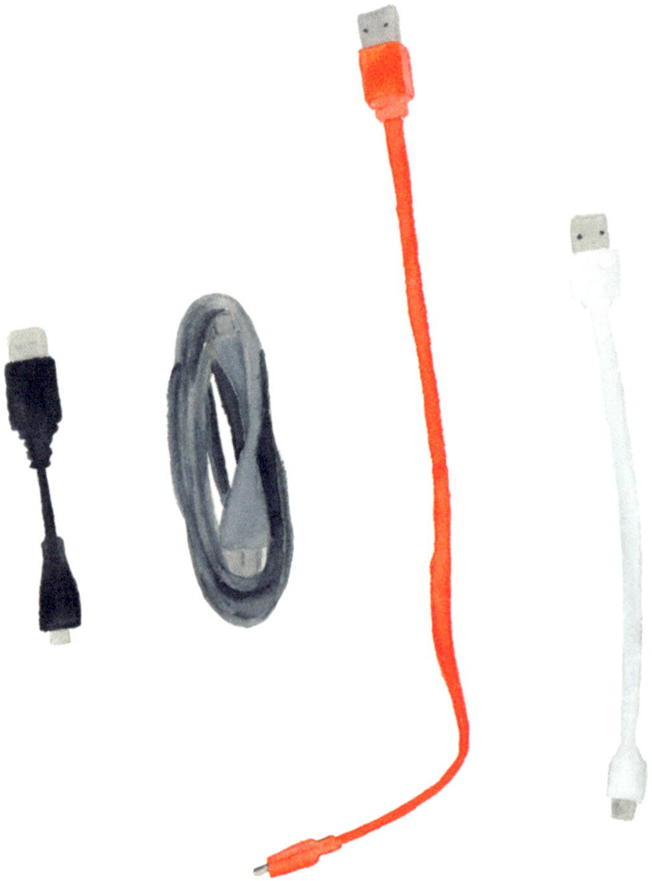

Cords

Binoculars

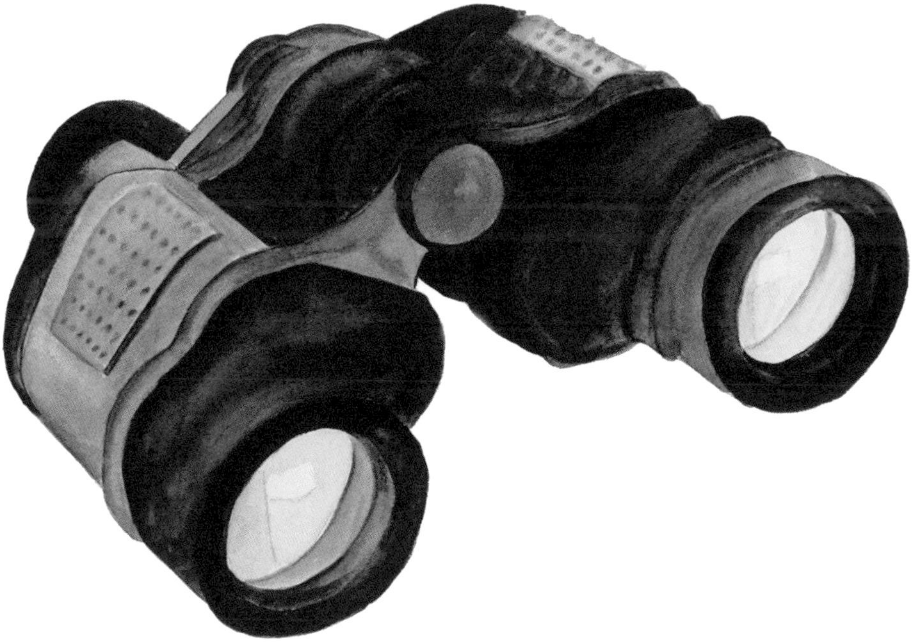

Flowering Under Stress

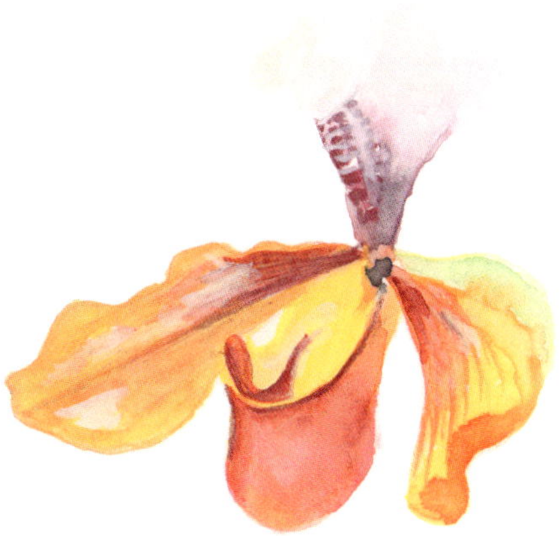

THIS IS A TIGER ORCHID.
IT FLOWERS ONLY UNDER
S T R E S S

Prehistoric

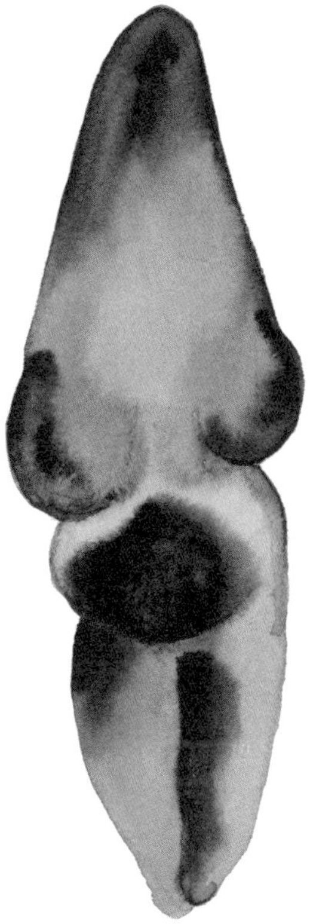

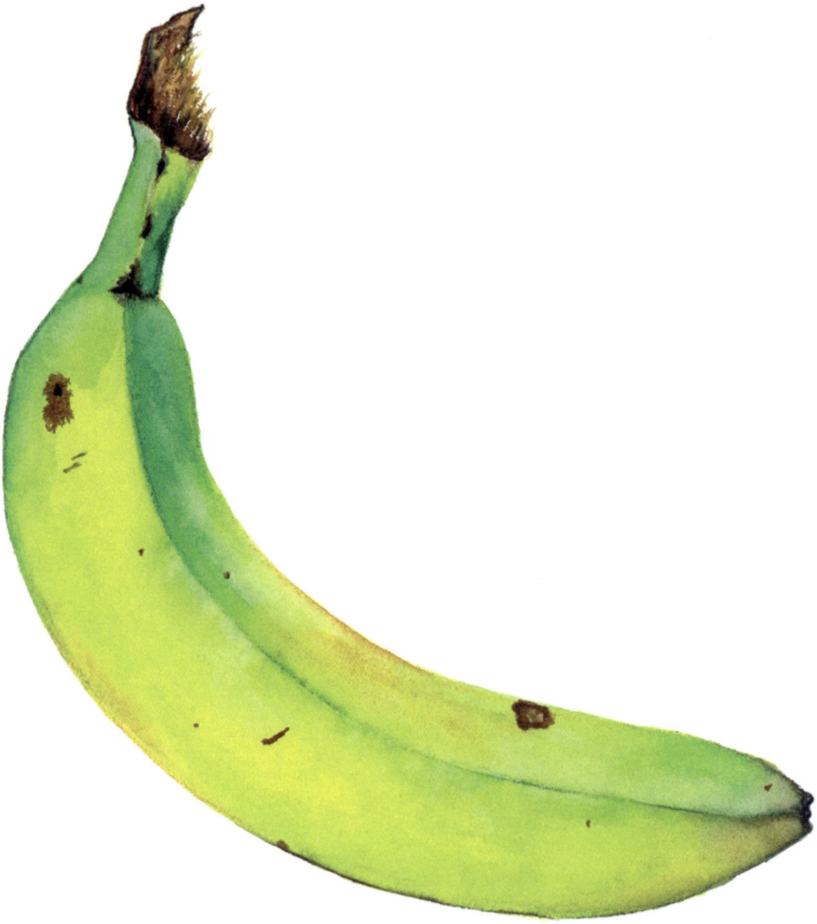

Banana

Tissue Box

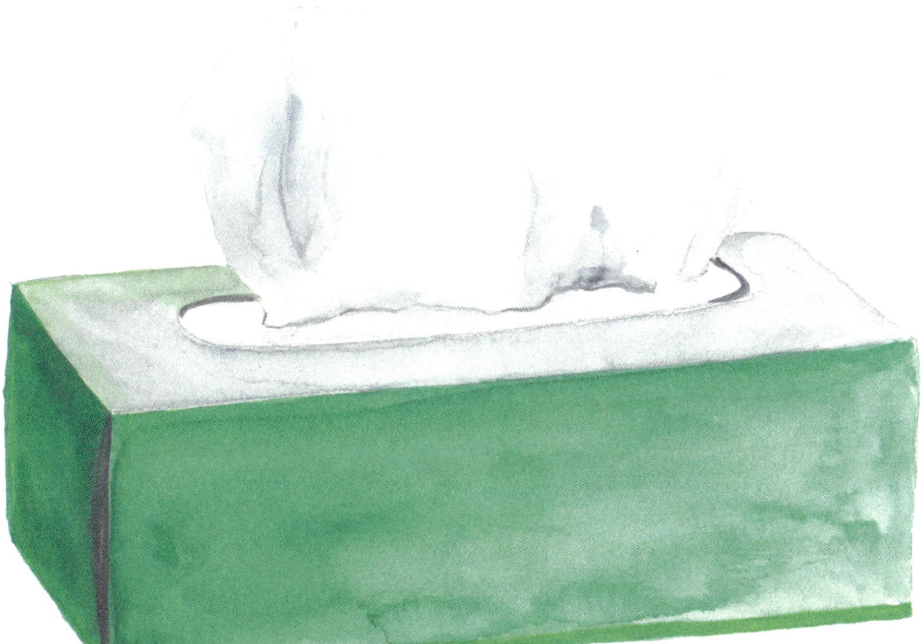

Vanilla Hominid

VANILLA HOMINID

Dormouse

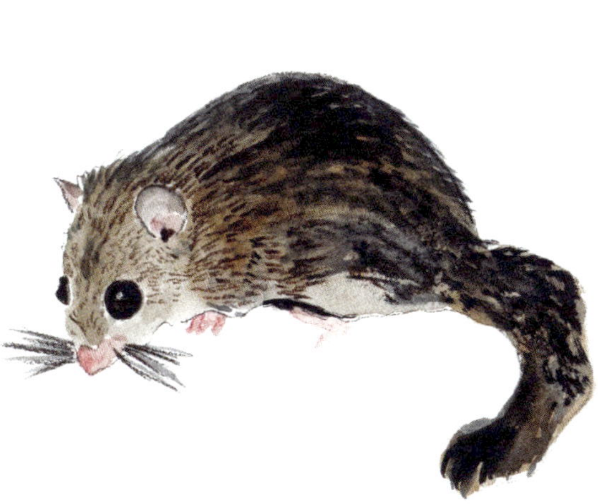

Self-Portrait as Super Glue

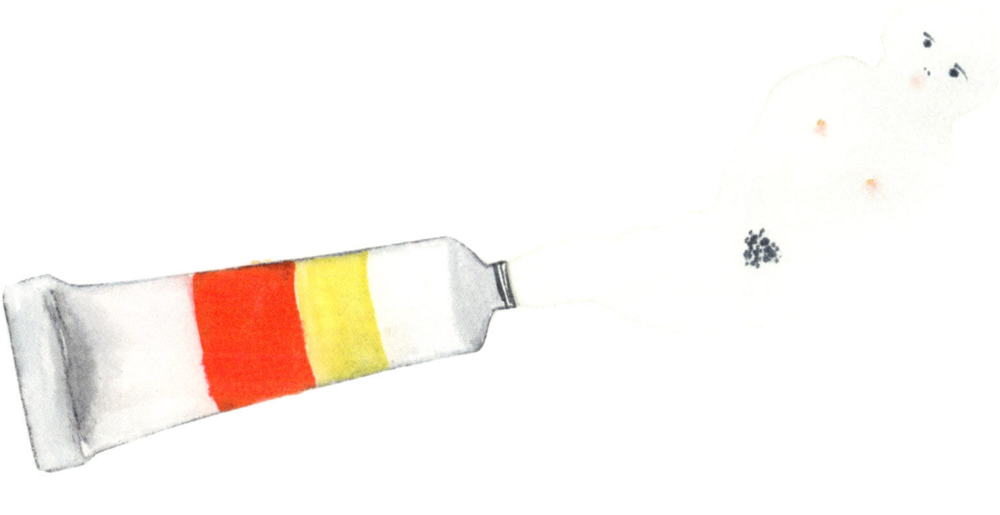

SELF PORTRAIT AS SUPER GLUE

Homeopathic Gesture

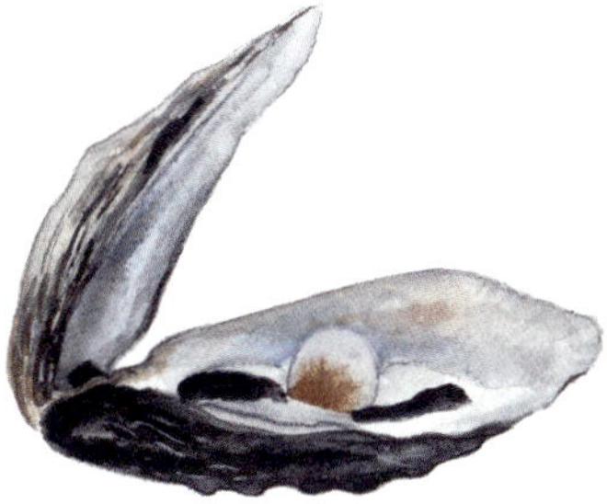

THE PEARL FORMS TO PROTECT THE OYSTER
FROM IRRITANTS SUCH AS SAND.
THE PEARL IS A HOMEOPATHIC GESTURE!

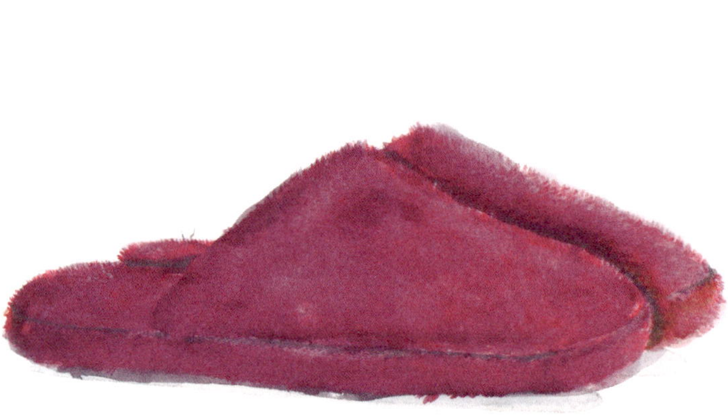

Purple Slippers

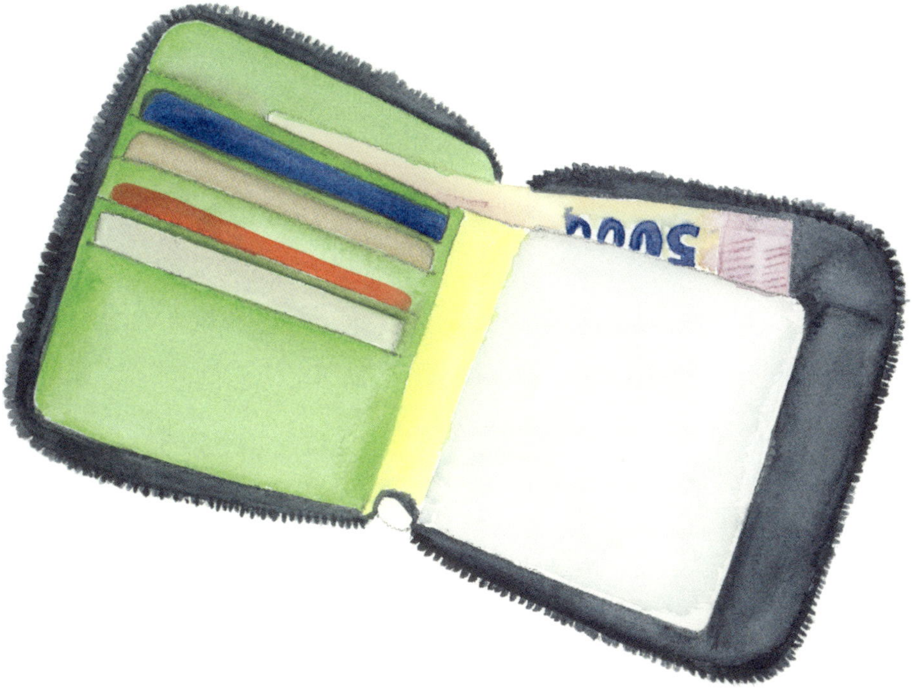

Wallet Portrait

Ancient Vegan Dessert

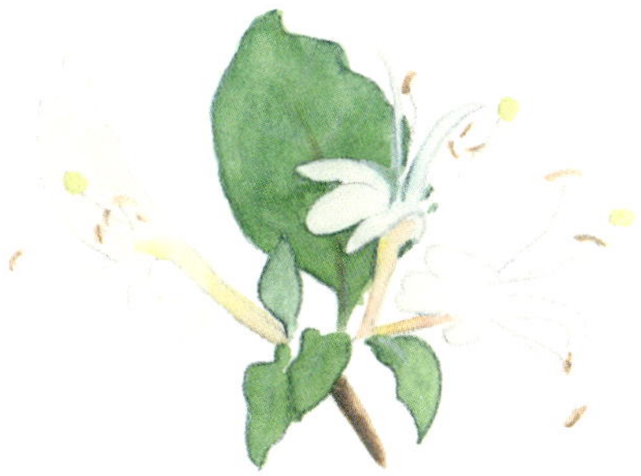

ANCIENT VEGAN DESSERT
(HONEYSUCKLE)

Self-Portrait

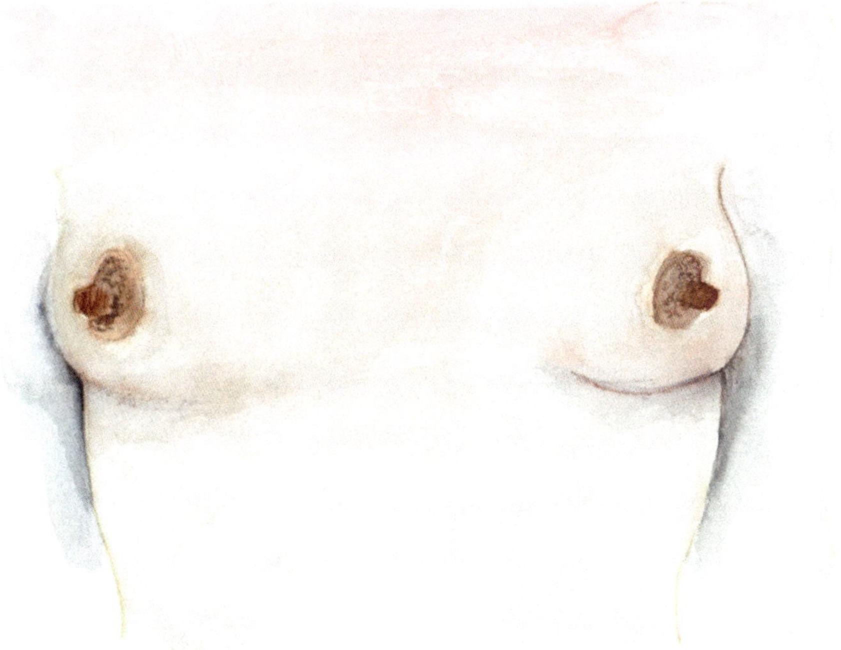

WHEN I WAS 4 I ASKED MY MOTHER TO EXPLAIN LACTATION.
SHE TOLD ME ONE BREAST MADE MILK, THE OTHER COFFEE, OR TEA.
HER ANSWER WAS FUNDAMENTAL IN HOW I BECAME WHO I AM.

Pillow (After Dürer)

Different Kinds of Dew

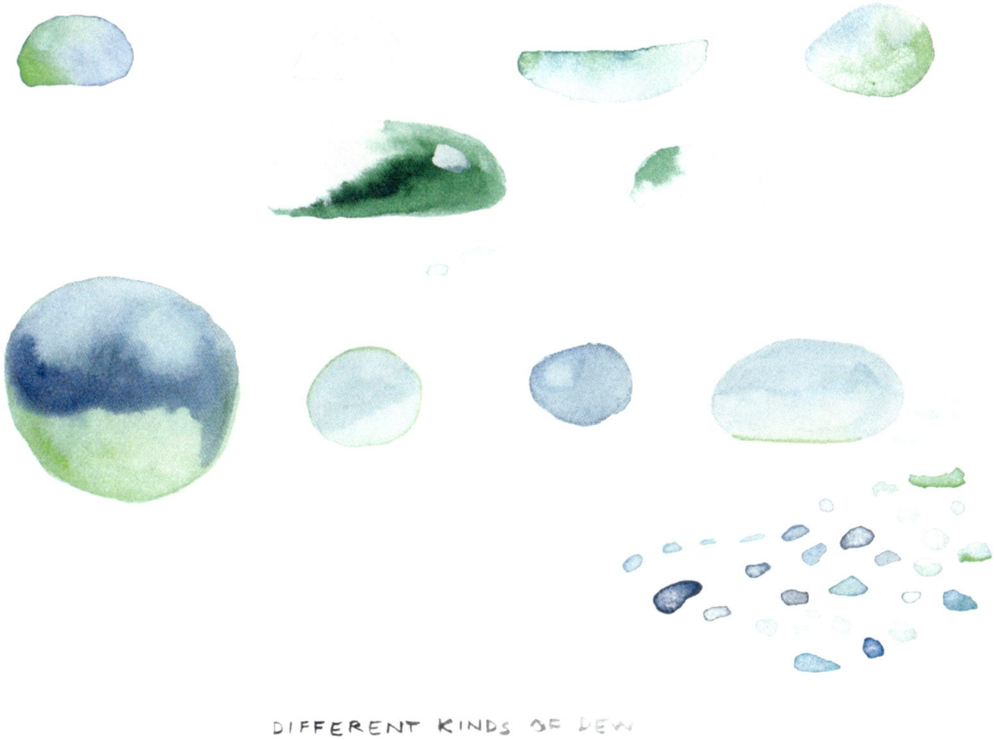

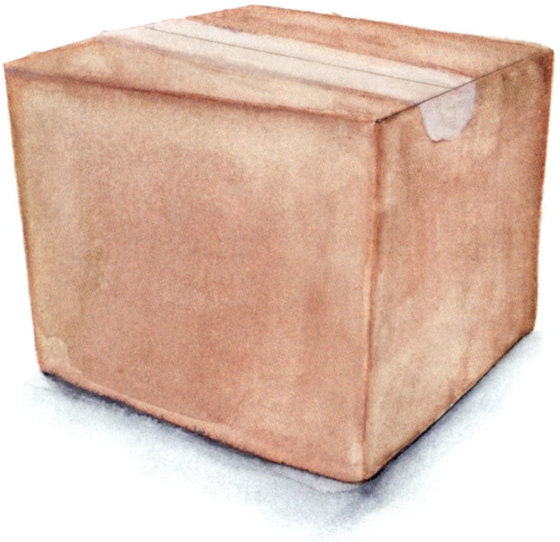

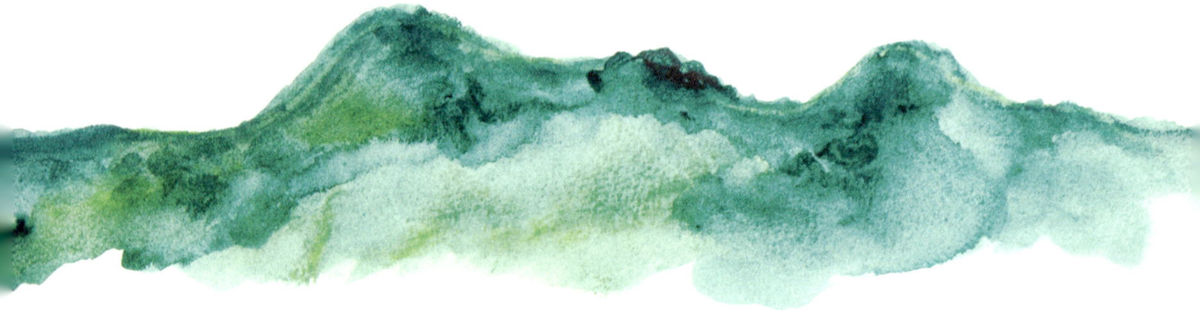

VERY GOOD FOR YOUR NERVOUS SYSTEM

Very Good for Your Nervous System

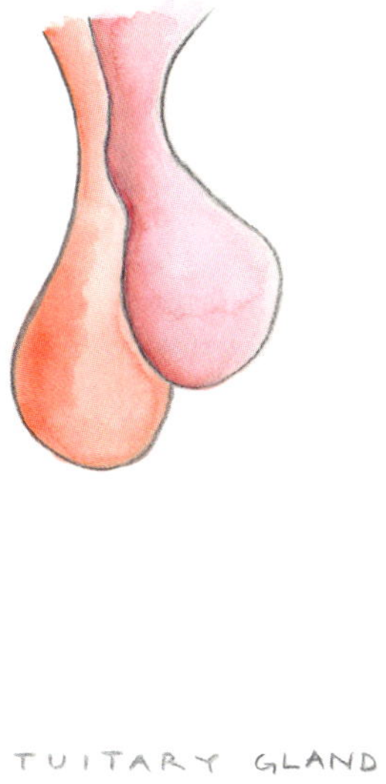

Pituitary Gland

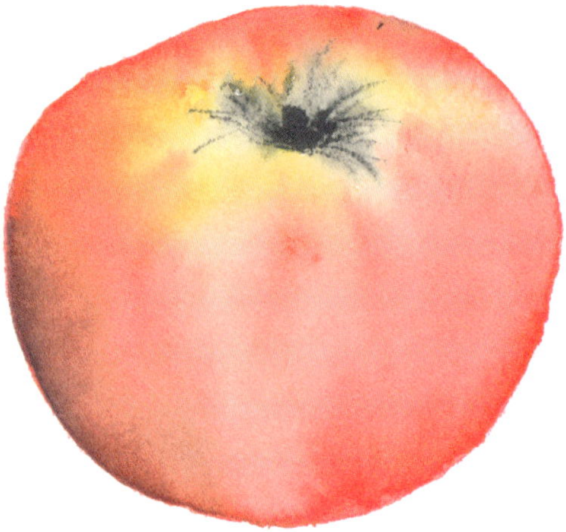

SWEAT INTO AN APPLE AND OFFER
IT TO YOUR BELOVED (MEDIEVAL GESTURE)

Apple Gesture

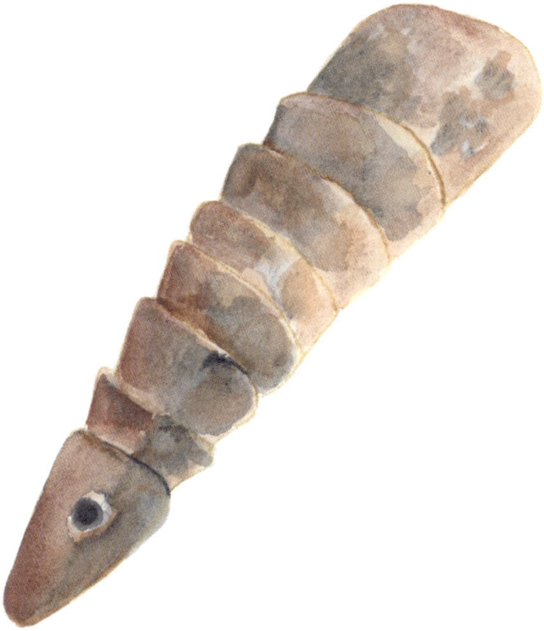

Wound Plug

Festina Lente

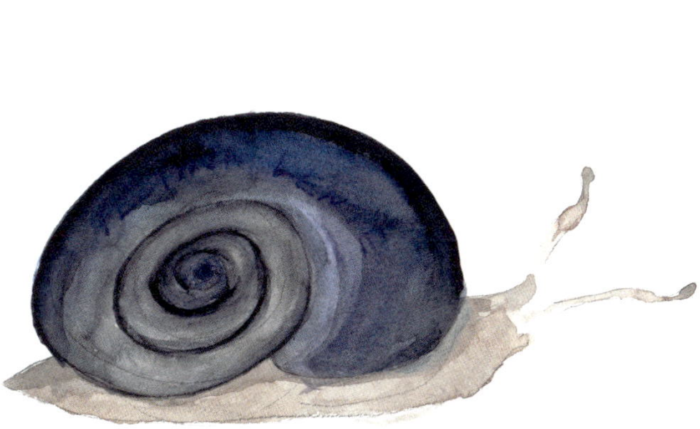

LIST OF WORKS

Support Shell, 2020
34 × 48 cm

Prehistoric, 2022
31 × 23 cm

Sexually Mature Queen, 2020
36 × 51 cm

Moss, 2022
31 × 41 cm

Playmate, 2022
31 × 41 cm

Zebra, 2023
51 × 36 cm

Wild Watercolor Fire, 2020
24 × 32 cm

Pinus Piñata, 2020
31 × 23 cm

Juvenile Swan, 2021
36 × 26 cm

Wallpaper with Mosquito Blood Pattern, 2020
24 × 32 cm

Virtual Hives are the New Cryptocurrency, 2021
36 × 26 cm

So Important for Your Nervous System, 2022
28 × 38 cm

Dexterity, 2022
31 × 41 cm

Bunny Ears, 2022
36 × 26 cm

Smoke, 2021
31 × 41 cm

Noah's Fridge, 2021
64 × 50 cm

The Airborne Future Requires Moisture to Live, 2020
34 × 48 cm

Sacrum and Coccyx with Neolithic Arrow, 2020
41 × 31 cm

Hell for Breakfast, 2021
31 × 41 cm

Lakes are Deeply Responsive, 2022
61 × 46 cm

So Sensitive, 2022
41 × 31 cm

Sleep Mask, 2022
31 × 41 cm

Delicately Vulgar, 2020
41 × 31 cm

Bee Wings, 2022
29.7 × 21 cm

Self-Portrait as Swiss Knife, 2021
41 × 31 cm

Hot Water Bottle, 2022
51 × 36 cm

Prehistoric Object, 2022
18 × 12.5 cm

Sexually Deceptive Pollination, 2020
21 × 16 cm

Self-Portrait as Espresso Pot, 2022
41 × 31 cm

Routine "Surpise," 2021
26 × 36 cm

Missing R, 2022
23 × 31 cm

Imaginary Scenario, 2022
26 × 18 cm

Radiator, 2023
120 × 80 cm

Work Only in Centimeters, 2022
51 × 36 cm

Swimming with Piglet, 2022
31 × 41 cm

Cords, 2023
40 × 30 cm

Bee Wing, 2022
29.7 × 21 cm

Watercolor Fire, 2022
31 × 41 cm

Prehistoric, 2022
18 × 12.5 cm

Tupperware, 2021
23 × 36 cm

Earplugs, 2022
31 × 23 cm

Squirrel, 2021
36 × 26 cm

Hybridchildren, 2022
23 × 31 cm

Self-Portrait as Blender, 2023
36 × 51 cm

Worker Female in Disguise as Sexually Mature Queen, 2021
23 × 31 cm

Parasol Mushroom, 2023
21 × 29.5 cm

Earth is Top-Heavy, 2022
36 × 51 cm

Kelp Eating Sheep, 2020
21.5 × 18 cm

Hip Fidget, 2023
29 × 21 cm

The Beekeeper (After Bruegel), 2023
30 × 40 cm

Sexually Mature Queen, 2021
36 × 26 cm

Emergency Queen, 2020
23 × 31 cm

Torrential Rain, 2022
76 × 106 cm

Burn Sadness Like Calories, 2020
24 × 32 cm

Something Good for Nervous System, 2022
28 × 38 cm

Marinating, 2020
30 × 21 cm

Moon Moving Away, 2020
34 × 48 cm

Mud Slides, 2022
63 × 45 cm

Orange Slippers, 2022
41 × 31 cm

Pillow (After Dürer), 2023
105 × 78 cm

Frying Pan, 2022
31 × 41 cm

Sage, 2022
29.7 × 21 cm

Bunny Ears, 2022
36 × 26 cm

Emergency Queen, 2022
26 × 36 cm

Pillow (After Dürer), 2022
21 × 29.7 cm

Spine, 2020
37.5 × 31 cm

Prawn, 2022
26 × 18 cm

Cords, 2023
46 × 36 cm

House Cat, 2022
41 × 31 cm

Self-Portrait as Pepper Grinder, 2022
41 × 31 cm

Honey Laundering, 2021
31 × 41 cm

Some Flowers Require Vibration, 2022
41 × 61 cm

Levity Rocks, 2021
41 × 31 cm

Languishing, 2020
24 × 32 cm

Egg, 2022
23 × 31 cm

Sheep Skin, 2022
41 × 31 cm

Early Hygiene Care, 2020
21 × 29.5 cm

Soup, 2020
18 × 26 cm

Cords, 2023
36 × 51 cm

Binoculars, 2022
31 × 41 cm

Flowering Under Stress, 2020
32 × 24 cm

Prehistoric, 2022
39 × 31 cm

Banana, 2021
36 × 26 cm

Tissue Box, 2022
41 × 31 cm

Vanilla Hominid, 2022
12.5 × 18 cm

Dormouse, 2022
31 × 23 cm

Self-Portrait as Super Glue, 2020
21.5 × 31 cm

Homeopathic Gesture, 2020
34 × 48 cm

Purple Slippers, 2022
41 × 31 cm

Wallet Portrait, 2022
36 × 51 cm

Ancient Vegan Dessert, 2022
26 × 18 cm

Self-Portrait, 2020
24 × 32 cm

Pillow (After Dürer), 2022
31 × 41 cm

Different Kinds of Dew, 2020
31 × 41 cm

(Untitled), 2021
32 × 24 cm

Very Good for Your Nervous System, 2022
28 × 38 cm

Pituitary Gland, 2020
26.5 × 24 cm

Apple Gesture, 2022
29.7 × 21 cm

Wound Plug, 2020
29.5 × 21 cm

Festina Lente, 2020
28 × 37 cm

Ana Prvački
FLOWERING UNDER STRESS

Published by	STERNBERG PRESS
Project manager	KSENIA JAKOBSON
Copy editor	STUART BERTOLOTTI-BAILEY
Proofreader	EMMA CAPPS
Design	WOLFE HALL
Printer	GRAPHIUS, BELGIUM

Flowering Under Stress was made possible with a grant from

STIFTUNG **KUNSTFONDS**

And has received generous support from LISA TUNG & SPENCER GLENDON and ARMYAN BERNSTEIN & CHRISTINE MELEO BERNSTEIN

Special thank you to CAROL LEWITT and the LEWITT FAMILY

ISBN 978-1-915609-26-7

Distributed by the MIT Press, Art Data, Les presses du réel, and Idea Books

Sternberg Press · 71–75 Shelton Street · London · WC2H 9JQ

sternberg-press.com